W9-CGX-691

Where Spirits Fly

the story of Camp Knutson

CAMP KNUTSON

"Camp Knutson is dedicated to nurturing the well-being of persons with special needs in a setting which celebrates God's love for community and creation."

During summer months (June through August) Camp Knutson is an accepting and nurturing camp environment for children with special needs.

Where Spirits Fly

the story of Camp Knutson

Pat Postlewaite
Karen Christofferson

photography by Beth Larson and Dan Mason

Camp Knutson

Camp Knutson Volunteers
Crosslake, Minnesota

for information, address
Camp Knutson Volunteers
11169 Whitefish Avenue
Crosslake, MN 56442

Layout and Design by Dorrie Simon, Studio 122
Principal photography by Beth Larson
Photo retouching by Suzanne Shaff, Suzanne Shaff Photography Worldwide
Photos on pages 34 and 37 used with permission of Lake County Echo
Printed in the United States of America by J-C Press

ISBN 978-0-692-23204-0

CAMP KNUTSON

Camp Knutson is a program of Lutheran Social Service of Minnesota that serves all people regardless of race, color, creed, religion, national origin, sex, sexual orientation, disability or age.

Contents

Acknowledgments

This book is the work of many. *Where Spirits Fly* was created because of Kathy Keeling's unflagging insistence that the story of Camp Knutson must be told and was made possible by Karen Christofferson's superb research. Her initial and engaging contacts resulted in submissions from nearly every person whose memories form this book. Pat Postlewaite wrote beautifully and was the "quilter" who gave the book its shape and context while stitching together the many pieces that tell Camp Knutson's remarkable story.

Camp director Rob Larson, assistant director Mary (Kate) Williams, and former director Dan Mason regularly provided encouragement and details about the workings and rich heart of the camp. Judy Morgan was the anchor who kept us grounded. Thank you to Beth Larson, Camp Knutson's "resident photographer," for sifting through hundreds of her compelling photos to show us the spirit of the camp, to Dan Mason for his vintage photos, to Chris Mattson, Lorraine Northagen, Emily Bilski, and Lutheran Social Service (LSS) and Camp Knutson staff for adding their photos, to Ed Brown for help in selecting photos, and to photographer Suzanne Shaff for her photo retouching.

We are grateful to LSS staff members Judith Becker, Mary Maguire, Ann Kirby McGill, and Mary Ella Pratte for their insightful recommendations and to JoAnn Braun, Judy Clarke, Kathy Keeling, and Judy Morgan for their diligent proofreading of each version of the emerging book. A particular thank you to Kara Pickman, freelance editor and former Camp Knutson summer staff, who generously provided the copy editing that put the final polish on the story. Graphic designer Dorrie Simon demonstrated exceptional creativity and patience during the design process. Thank you.

An especially warm thank you to the following people who were interviewed or wrote to us about their passion for Camp Knutson: _Camp Directors_ Andy Boe, Reub Jessop, Rob Lane, Gordon Long, Dan Mason, Michael Muehlbach, JoAnn Donner Peterson, and Ray Runkel; _Representatives of the 2014 Participating Camps_ Terri Borowick and Wendy McNeil, Autism Society of Minnesota; Angie Kniss, Down Syndrome Foundation; Sara Meslow, Camp Odayin; Connie Statz, Camp Benedict; Al Bostlemann and members of the Minneapolis Community Group; and Dr. Mark Dahl and Janine Mueller, American Academy of Dermatology; _Former Staff and Board of LSS_ Dan Bergelund, Eleanor Goodall, Mark Peterson, Dayton Soby and Bob York; _Volunteers_ Kay Antos, Jerry and Sandy Bilski, Sue Buchite, Jesse Eide, Rev. Dick Erickson, Fr. Paul Fruth, Nancy Thayer Haggerty, Rene Hanning, Kathy Morgan, Gail Peterson, Betsy Simons, Dan Thorson, Susann Zeug-Hoese; and _Former Camp Staff_ Erik Anderson, Becca Bjorke, Kjersten Grinde, Robalee Kjelland, Kate Kubat, Caitlin Malin, Quinn Meyer, Andrew Million, Jake Wessels, Whitney Keltner-Wessels, and Marie Wilson.

A final thank you to anyone we may have missed. You know your importance in this project and in the post-production work required. It was a privilege and life-changing experience for us to be involved in this volunteer effort.

Book Committee

Preface

Camp Knutson changes lives. Scores of letters sent to camp from campers, parents, and community members say so. Following a weeklong camp session for children with skin diseases, one parent wrote:

This was the first time that our daughter traveled without either of her parents. She cried boarding the flight, filled with apprehension. However, I am pleased to report that she cried even more at the end of her camping week because she had so much fun and had to leave all her friends and supporters behind! Two grateful parents want you to know that the work you do at camp is a 'game change' in the lives of these kids who are trying to make sure they fit into an imperfect world. Thank you for all you do.

In May 1954, Camp Knutson opened its doors to children and youth unable to attend any other camp—children living with developmental disabilities, inner-city youth living in poverty, children with vision and hearing impairments, and "troubled boys" living in residential treatment centers. At camp, surrounded by total acceptance during the day and loon calls at night, the children experienced their own "game change."

During summer 2014, Camp Knutson will serve close to 1,100 individuals—650 children with unique needs related to heart disease, skin disorders, autism, Down syndrome, and HIV/AIDS, accompanied by 450 specially trained support staff.

Some of these children face challenges similar to those of eleven-year-old Soren. When Soren was a newcomer at Camp Knutson, he fell in love with the waterfront. Soren has had three heart surgeries. He remembers being airlifted from his hometown hospital to a major children's hospital. "I got lucky and survived," he said. "I thought I wouldn't make it. I'm missing a quarter of my heart." Now, Soren says the night before he comes to camp his heart starts to race. "I'm excited and nervous at the same time. I just want to get there so bad. I want to get there early and go check out the beach." Soren knows how to pace his exertion at camp. He sports a slight, proud grin when he talks about riding the golf cart up the long hill from the waterfront.

Where Spirits Fly is an abbreviated history of Camp Knutson's sixty-one years. It celebrates the camp's mission of changing lives, the kids it serves, and the grassroots efforts that keep it vital. The book contains a number of terms for disabling conditions that are no longer in use today; these terms were included to maintain the integrity of the historical writings from which they were derived. The book also details memories of many individuals' involvement with camp, a mere glimpse of the thousands of stories that exist. If the story of your involvement with Camp Knutson is not included, please know it is carried with gratitude in so many hearts.

Camp Knutson is a joyful place. It is a magical place. *Where Spirits Fly* will show you why.

Book Committee:
Karen Christofferson, Volunteer

Kathy Keeling, Volunteer

Judy Morgan, Volunteer

Pat Postlewaite, Volunteer

Rob Larson, Director, Camp Knutson

Mary (Kate) Williams, Assistant Director, Camp Knutson

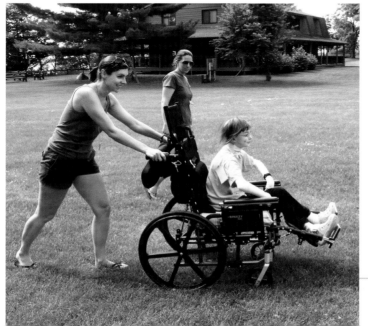

Introduction

Camp Knutson sits on thirty acres of pristine property "up north" in northern Minnesota, on a peninsula of land between Big Trout Lake and Whitefish Lake, two popular lakes on the Whitefish Chain. Nearly thirty miles north of Brainerd, this chain of lakes was created by the Army Corps of Engineers, initially to keep the Mississippi River navigable downstream, and later, to promote sportfishing and tourism in this area.

For centuries, people have cherished the area and considered it to be life-giving. The land was held sacred for its beauty and abundance by the Ojibwa and Dakota, who traveled the area's lakes and rivers and seasonally settled on its banks to fish and hunt. By 1871, lumbering flourished there, and soon as many as 1,400 lumberjacks bunked in barracks less than five miles away from Camp Knutson's property. In the early 1900s, lumbering declined and tourism began to advance. People were drawn to the area for recreation and to experience nature's restorative calm.

The land we know today as Camp Knutson was once owned by the United States government and logged for its valuable timber. The property was bought in 1922 and changed hands once more before being sold, in 1942, to Congressman Harold Knutson. Knutson had vacationed on the peninsula with family members and friends beginning in 1921. Today the land is owned by Lutheran Social Service of Minnesota.

From the Director

On a cold January day, some twenty-five years ago, I made my first visit to Camp Knutson. I parked near the entrance of camp and trudged through knee-deep snow down the driveway and into the heart of the camp. Camp Knutson was closed for the winter, and the buildings were cold and locked down. Equipped with a big set of keys, I made my way around, visiting the dining hall, Hilltop Cabin, camper cabins, and the boathouse. From that very first day I knew that Camp Knutson was a spectacular place and that being the new director would be a tremendous opportunity for me and my family. What I didn't know at that time was how important camp was and is to the hundreds of campers, families, staff, and volunteers who have set foot on these sacred grounds.

The 1990s was a time of strategic planning as we looked for ways to keep Camp Knutson viable. For all of us involved, this demanded a deep look into the camp's history to understand what it has meant for campers and how

the place—the acreage here at Camp Knutson—is truly special. As director, I have been given the opportunity to be involved with all aspects of camp life, to witness the evolution of camp, and to work closely with camp's dedicated advisory council. In recent years, I have seen Camp Knutson transform. The revitalization of camp facilities goes hand in hand with the growth of its programming and the involvement of hundreds of volunteers, donors, staff, and campers.

As I look back at recent events, highlights include the 50th anniversary in August 2003 and the *Rebuilding for*

Left page: Kate Williams, Assistant Director, and Rob Larson, Director, pose as reindeer in front of camp logo.

Good campaign that modernized the entire camp facilities and grounds. The support and encouragement we have received from Jerry and Sandy Bilski, the co-chairs of this campaign, have truly been a blessing to Camp Knutson and the children we serve. It has been a wonderful experience to work with the Paul Bunyan Region Auxiliary of Lutheran Social Service to put on the annual Camp Knutson Quilt Auction and to work with the Camp Knutson volunteers who participate in nearly every aspect of daily camp life and help raise much-needed funds. We have so many talented volunteers and groups of volunteers, such as the Friends of Camp Knutson, who have embraced the mission of camp and truly made it their own.

Another highlight has been the development and growth of camp's programming under the guidance and leadership of Mary (Kate) Williams, Assistant Director. Working with Kate has been a privilege; her enthusiasm and endless energy is a powerful motivator for all of us. Kate's work with our college-age program staff is extraordinary; her mentorship of these young people is truly a gift. To witness the multitude of campers and staff who have participated in recent years is a dream come true.

Today, as I sit here in the Hilltop Cabin overlooking Whitefish Lake, I'm reminded of the peaceful and restorative nature of Camp Knutson and everyone it touches. It has taken an immeasurable amount of time and energy from talented and dedicated people and our courageous campers to make Camp Knutson what it is today. For me, it has been a remarkable journey that I'm honored to be a part of; it has been the ride of a lifetime and I'm truly thankful to God that Camp Knutson has been my home for these many years. I'm pleased to offer a closer look at this camp and the lives that are changed here.

Rob Larson, Director
Crosslake, Minnesota
March 2014

From Dream to Reality

Our Origins

Photo by Sathers of Brainerd, Minn.

In August 1953, former Minnesota Congressman Harold Knutson finalized nearly two years of planning by deeding his beloved summertime retreat, Dunworkin', to the Evangelical Lutheran Church. His intentions were specific—his cottage and thirty acres of lakeshore property thirty miles north of Brainerd, MN were to be used "exclusively as a summer retreat for neglected, unfortunate, deprived and handicapped children during the months of June, July, and August each year." The camp was to be a living memorial to his mother, Jeanette Holm Knutson, whom he dearly loved.

Harold was born in Skien, Norway in 1880. His family moved to the United States when he was six, first settling in Chicago but later moving near St. Cloud, MN, where his parents struggled to make a meager living as farmers. At age twenty-two, Knutson left the farm and apprenticed in the printing business with a newspaper in Royalton, MN, sleeping in a room over the shop. He eventually bought that paper and the *Wadena Pioneer Journal*, sixty-eight miles away, launching a lifelong career in publishing.

A Republican, Knutson was elected to Congress from his central Minnesota district in 1916, succeeding C.A. Lindbergh, the father of aviator Charles Lindbergh. When Knutson was defeated for re-election in 1948, he returned to the *Wadena Pioneer Journal,* where he worked until his death in 1953.

Harold Knutson seated with children. Printed in *Lutheran Herald*, October 6, 1953.

Portrait of Harold Knutson, in the Collection of U.S. House of Representatives, painted by Thomas Stephens.

In Congress, Knutson was, at various times, Republican Whip, Chair of the Ways and Means Committee, and member of the Joint Commission on Reduction of Nonessential Federal Expenditures.

Minneapolis Star-Tribune writer Robert Franklin wrote of Knutson as: *"a cigar-smoking bachelor with a fondness for salads, steaks, high tariffs and tax cuts. He sponsored reforestation legislation, voted against U.S. entry into World War I and worked to keep the nation out of World War II before Pearl Harbor. As chairman of the House Ways and Means Committee, he pushed through a tax-cut bill over vetoes by President Harry Truman."*

Knutson was known for his sharp tongue felt by colleagues on both sides of the political aisle. Dick Robertson, a writer from the *Wadena Pioneer Journal*, wrote: *"Knutson has been variously portrayed as a villain and a saint—as a heartless manservant of privilege, a hardboiled fighter for the common man, an arrogant exponent of outmoded isolationism, a vigorous spokesman in the good fight against foreign "isms," a mischievous guardian of oppressive wealth, a courageous champion of honest-to-Betsy Americanism..."*

In his childhood, Knutson's family had only the barest of life's necessities and few opportunities for recreation; they longed for the opportunities Knutson later found with friends and relatives at 'Dunworkin'. On August 15, 1953, Harold Knutson suffered a series of heart attacks and died, on August 21, just two days before the opening dedication of Camp Knutson.

For the camp dedication ceremony, Harold's brother-in-law, the Reverend Alfred Bredesen of Venice, Florida, sent a tape recording, excerpted on far right, in which he narrated a full biography of Harold's mother Jeanette.

Today, the camp that would have been so dear to Jeannette's heart is owned and operated by Lutheran Social Service of Minnesota (LSS), an organization that traces its roots back to Vasa Children's Home of Red Wing, Minnesota, established in 1865 to care for children orphaned "through illness, the severe struggle of crossing an ocean and a continent, Indian uprisings, and the rigors of frontier life."

The events that culminated in Knutson deeding his land to the Evangelical Lutheran Church first began in conversations with his brother-in-law. Knutson spoke with Bredesen about perhaps leaving his land "to someone who would evidence a spirit of responsibility" as he wanted to memorialize his mother and keep alive the Knutson family name. Below, a summary of an August 14, 1953 radio address by Reverend Magnus Dahlen, Executive Secretary to the Board of Charities of the Evangelical Lutheran Church, chronicles the steps leading to the transfer of Knutson's land.

In early 1952	Dr. O.G. Malmin, editor of *Lutheran Herald*, receives a personal letter from Bredesen summarizing Knutson's intentions to donate lakeshore property to a worthy cause. Malmin visits office of Board of Charities suggesting Dahlen "certainly think what such an opportunity might present."
May 19, 1952	Dahlen and wife visit the Knutson property. Dahlen comments that "he would so much wish that this could become the property of his church for a useful and spirited program for someone some day."
July 1, 1952	Dahlen calls on Knutson at *Wadena Pioneer Journal* and describes the programs of the Department of Charities. States dreams of a Minnesota place of retreat for "children who by circumstances have been neglected, handicapped and deprived." Knutson writes a simple statement of intent.
July 19, 1952	Dahlen, members of Board of Charities, members' wives and other interested persons visit Knutson at the property and discuss hopes for camp. They view slides of "activities in the Charities and Welfare field from Coast to Coast and up into Canada"—children's homes, homes for the aged, child placing and foster programs, and institutional chaplaincy programs.
August 25, 1952	Dahlen visits Knutson in Wadena. Is instructed to proceed to draw up agreement. Knutson leaving for Florida mid-September, stated he would like all things completed by the end of year.

Jeannette and her husband, Christian, … emigrated to America in 1886 with their four children, the youngest a baby in arms… Here (near St. Cloud) in a pioneer farm community, they shared the common lot of struggle and privation. They were ill prepared for such conditions. Their main resources were the intangible riches of industry and frugality, and the faith that God is the rewarder of those who diligently seek Him. She often thanked God for America. Here, alone, her family saga could have unfolded. There are only a few real satisfactions in life. Here in America, the Christian Knutson family found and won them all.

…The deep undertone of the life of Jeannette Holm Knutson was her simple childlike faith in her Savior. The worn Bible was never far away. Part of the song of her life was written in the minor key of want and privation, but all jarring discords gradually blended into the beautiful symphony of joy and gratitude to Him who justified her faith and fulfilled her dearest hopes…

It is very appropriate that the Jeannette Holm Knutson camp for underprivileged children should be her memorial. She believed in the association of all who loved in the service of all who suffer. May God bless her memorial and the love that made it possible.

— Alfred Bredesen, 1953
Camp Knutson dedication

"Oh, you know," said Mr. Knutson, "I could have sold this point out here a thousand times. There was the man from Texas with oil holdings who came by and laid down a check of $35,000 but I wouldn't take it. Then he took his check book and said, 'You fill in the amount'—but no."

Laying the Foundation

When Reverend Magnus Dahlen was deeded the Knutson property, he assigned his assistant, Reverend John Mason, to move Camp Knutson from dream to reality.

The Board of Charities maintained a number of children's homes throughout Minnesota, North and South Dakota, Iowa and Wisconsin for children considered "unfortunate, deprived, and handicapped." These became the first stream of children to experience the delight of the camp Harold Knutson dreamt would occupy his cherished property.

By design, Camp Knutson would provide lodging, use of a kitchen, and a staff to direct waterfront activities, games, nature-based and craft activities, and evening songs around a camp fire. The guest camping group was to bring their own cook and food, bedding, staff in numbers sufficient to provide twenty-four-hour supervision of their campers, and their own therapeutic program.

With "love of neighbor" as its guiding principle, Camp Knutson aimed to meet the specific needs of each camper group it hosted, creating a welcoming environment that would accept and celebrate each participant. The camp became a place where those who sit at the edge of the circle were brought to the center, where attention and respect were given to those who were used to being on the margins. Its philosophy of care was developed, not in planning sessions, but in the experiences with the campers themselves.

Campers enjoy a campfire at Camp Knutson in the 1950s.

Bright Eager Faces
Ray Runkel, Director, 1954

Ray Runkel was a seminary student and assistant youth-center director, intending to work with inner city youth in Chicago that summer, when Reverend Dahlen asked him to direct the camp. In 1954, Camp Knutson's first summer in operation, it was host to children living in six group homes located in Minnesota and other surrounding states. "I'd always liked camping," Runkel recalled, "and my Plymouth youth group was already planning to be at Camp Knutson, so it was an easy decision." In a letter from the Board of Charities dated May 25, 1954,

Runkel's position was described as "program co-ordinator, chaplain and in charge of everything pertaining to the supervision of water activity."

When his classes ended in May, Runkel headed out in a 1937 Chevrolet to visit the group homes scheduled to attend camp that summer. He wanted to meet with the staff and children, become a familiar face, and learn the camper needs for each group. Along the way, Runkel collected equipment to use at the camp and whatever the institutions could contribute—towels, bed linens, blankets and pots and pans.

In an archived report of the summer, Runkel noted that when the Plymouth Christian Youth Center in Minneapolis brought a group of eighteen to camp, three boys on probation from the St. Paul Court joined the group. The three boys "proved to be of good assistance, being older and willing to take responsibility."

Runkel further noted that when a group of fifty campers and twenty staff from Beloit Children's Home from Ames, Iowa came to camp, conditions were "crowded." In addition to the camp's dormitories, three tents were pitched and cots were set up in the garage to accommodate everyone.

Children's homes visited by the camp director prior to the start of the 1954 camp season. He sought to become a familiar face so the children would be comfortable when they came to camp.

Lutheran Children's Home	St. Paul, MN
Lutheran Children's Home	Fergus Falls, MN
Svee Children's Home	Fargo, ND
Lutheran Children's Home	Beresford, SD
Lutheran Home for Children	Ames, IA
Lutheran Children's Home	Stoughton, WI

The final group of campers that summer came from Fargo, North Dakota, from the Nelle Svee Children's Home. Runkel described them as "an excellent group of children with willing hands who worked hard at completing the unfinished projects of previous camps. Campfire singing and bright eager faces, always desiring new avenues to explore, characterized this fine camp."

Making Camp
Rueben Jessop, Director, 1955-56

When Rueben Jessop was hired to direct camp in the spring of 1955, he and a friend spent a long weekend before camp's opening repairing the boat house, garage, and outdoor toilets, as well as constructing outdoor wash stands.

Jessop married in mid-June and one week later, he and his wife opened camp with a core staff of seven—Jessop as director, his wife as craft director, the cook and maintenance person who were returnees from the camp's first year, a nurse, a waterfront director, and an assistant volunteer craft person.

At that time, the home of Congressman Knutson was not available for camp use so the building known as the "duplex," Knutson's former office, was pressed into service. The upper level was used as Jessop's office and living quarters for the Jessops, the nurse, and the nurse's assistant; its bottom floor was divided into two dormitory areas. The building had one small bathroom.

Cook Anna Kindem put together a smorgasbord each Friday for supper including her famous lefse.

Camp Knutson

Above: Temporary dining hall. Center: Early postcard shows dining hall built in 1959.

The camp had a temporary dining hall and kitchen and a small garage that was used for craft activities. The boat house, used for storing waterfront equipment and dock sections, also housed the waterfront director. Outdoor toilets and wash-stands completed the camp's accommodations.

During the summer of 1955, a campfire area was pre-pared on the point by staff and campers, and space to accommodate a ball field and athletic area was cleared by bulldozer at a cost of $125. A boat, motor and pair of water skis were purchased and the camp received official certification by the State of Minnesota.

In 1956, the children's-home groups that had come to Camp Knutson returned for another season. In addition, the Plymouth Youth Center from Minneapolis conducted two week-long sessions with approximately seventy-five children each session; it became necessary to construct tent platforms to hold tents and beds for campers. Work that summer revolved around preparing the tent plat-forms and creating rifle and archery ranges. Tents, beds and mattresses were the camps major purchases.

Our Bethesda by the Sea
Gordon Long, Director, 1961, 1963-65

Gordon Long took a friend's advice and applied to be Camp Knutson's waterfront director in 1957; he later spent seven more summers at camp. About his first summer as an eighteen-year-old, Long later wrote:

"One day after lunch, I was working on a boat alone on the waterfront, when Reverend Magnus Dahlen, who had been central in facilitating the gift of land from Congressman Harold Knutson, strolled across the beach.

He sat down on the boathouse concrete apron, removed his shoes and socks, rolled up his suit pants and waded ankle deep around the edge of the swimming area. He didn't seem to mind his incongruous appearance in this setting—white shirt and tie, dress pants rolled up to his knees. His gaze was distant as he enjoyed a quiet

Boathouse and view to Big Trout lake.
Photo inset:
Swimmers enjoy the beach in 1955.

Gordon Long
doing paperwork
in boathouse
accommodations and
improving sailing skills
on Trout Lake.

moment wading in the cool water. He mused aloud, in a deep Scandinavian brogue, 'This Knutson Camp is our *Bethesda by the Sea.'*

I didn't know of any Bethesda by the sea, and assumed it was some biblical town of rare beauty, that at long last this camp fulfilled a vision for the use of an extraordinary piece of land. But the beauty he referred to was more than that of the land, for the scriptural Bethesda was a place of healing for body and of soul, especially sought by those called 'invalid,' who had been, because of their condition, left at society's margins. Camp Knutson would

have that precise calling—a place of healing for body and soul for children with special needs.

And how did that healing of body and soul play out? On that same waterfront the mother of a developmentally disabled adult son would say, 'We can go to any beach in the Twin Cities and endure the intentional distance of other beach goers, but here we enjoy one another's company because we all belong.'

Here, also, campers from the church's children's homes would try out the canoes, at first inevitably going around *in circles, but eventually learning it was possible to paddle straight across the lake, into the bay, through the culvert and back to the hidden magic of the most beautiful lagoon, shaded by tall pines, bordered by purple iris, dotted by water lilies, where they were apt to see the great blue heron, or deer emerging from the forest for a drink.*

There would be overnight camping trips to the island—rain, shine and mosquitoes—with children from a Minneapolis outreach program for children of impoverished economic means. There would be fishing trips for the elusive bluegill with children from the Family Counseling Unit of Lutheran Welfare. There would be sailboat rides, where for the first time one would hear called with earnestness, 'Coming about!' meaning 'watch out for the boom,' then experience the excitement of the boat heeling up on the opposite side. And behind it all would be the healing hand of the One who long ago told a lame man to 'rise, take up your bed and walk.'

Later on in the summer of 1957, to that Knutson waterfront area a chaplain from Ephphatha Services—a mission to children who were hearing impaired or who were visually impaired—would bring his own speedboat and spend hours teaching campers how to waterski for the

first time. One week he communicated in sign language to deaf children, the next week he patiently taught blind children how to manage the pull of the rope and anticipate crossing the boat's wake.

He then explained to the lifeguard how teachers back at the Minnesota School for the Deaf or from the Minnesota School for the Blind would remark about the increase in self esteem and self confidence that was apparent in the classroom stemming from this seemingly unrelated experience of learning to master standing up on waterskis at a camp called Knutson."

Visually impaired camper wanting one more goodbye.

Postcard with aerial view of Whitefish Peninsula showing Camp Knutson property.

A Daily Feeling of Joy
Andy Boe, Director, 1966-67

Just after high school graduation, Andy Boe headed to Camp Knutson as a lifeguard at the encouragement of his father, Paul Boe, Executive Director of the Division of Charities, whose task it was to oversee Camp Knutson.

Boe spent four years on the waterfront and then directed camp for an additional two years. According to Boe:

"The waterfront was the heart of the camp. We had a short time for swim lessons, followed by free swim and then the use of the canoes, rowboats, and our sailboat. Our old, donated runabout had a 35 HP motor that could barely move the boat, but it worked well enough to pull water skiers. Many days I pulled kids all afternoon and then again after supper—for six to eight hours.

I remember so well one girl from waterfront. She was probably twelve. She was deaf and had very active cerebral palsy that made it hard for her to use sign language or to swim. But she had a crush on me, a very sweet and innocent crush, and she worked especially hard every day in swim lessons and free swim to please me. When she left camp at the end of ten days, she was truly improved. By then, my opinion mattered much less because she was so proud of what she had accomplished."

Boe was married in the early summer of 1966, during his first year as camp director. He and his wife Joan chose to spend their honeymoon at the camp: "When we arrived on the Monday after our wedding, fifty or so campers from Lake Park-Wild Rice Children's Home were wildly ringing the bell and cheering us back to another great summer at camp."

Boe remembers a daily feeling of joy at camp. "The children reveled in the beauty of nature and the outdoor activities. With our combined staffs they got much more individual attention. They became kids again, less serious or withdrawn. They laughed and played. Even the boys had fun being silly." When new campers or staff came to Camp Knutson, looking out over the full expanse of Whitefish Lake was beyond what many had ever seen. "We never got tired of that view," Boe said. "The sky changed in appearance many times each day."

At the close of each camping group's session, there was a talent show that ended with awards. "Every single child was individually called forward and presented an award," Boe said. "It might say, 'You have a great smile' or 'You have wonderful things to say,' but whatever it said, the comments were specific and true—both staff and campers had recognized them. There was a real sense of community affection that final night."

Camper Reports
Dan Mason, Director, 1968-79

Having volunteered at Camp Knutson at age sixteen and later worked on summer staff, Dan Mason knew the camp served a worthy cause and was a fun place to work. When he became director in 1968, Mason was on faculty in the art department at Bethany College in Kansas. In a 1977 end-of-season report, Mason noted the emotions connected with closing down camp for the season:

"During our closing-up days we will be very busy, working at a multitude of tasks that express our caring for Camp Knutson. We will work each day well into the evening renewing the cabins, scraping and painting the boats and dock, refinishing the dining hall floor, and we will be tired. But we know that this, too, is part of the experience of love that is Camp Knutson. We have met so many new friends who are retarded, disturbed, blind, deaf, or mentally ill, and we realize how much their struggle for life is one of dignity and worth, and how their brief contact with us has enhanced our lives. And we know that, as we work, we are making the first preparations for next year, when the bell will ring again, and we, or those who follow us, will begin again to discover the joys of Camp Knutson and its people."

Mason's report also offers a glimpse of the typical camp morning. Breakfast announcements deal largely with the many choices of activities available: group fishing on the pontoon boat after first digging worms, canoe lessons and a group trip through the lagoon, making photos with Polaroid cameras, archery, tie-dyeing, movie making, and hiking to look for raspberries. These small groups of campers would accumulate experiences to bring back to the whole group in their lunchtime camper reports.

Camp Knutson staff member Michael Muehlbach helping a camper with a report in the dining hall.

Camper Reports

We often say that the basis of the Camp Knutson program is support and recognition of individuals. One of the most effective ways recognition is achieved is through camper reports which follow each meal. Campers are invited to stand up and tell us about what they have done since the last time the group was together. It is an important moment in camp life. Michael Muehlbach is very skilled at helping hesitant campers express themselves, or interpreting speech that is difficult to understand. The process takes time; it is not efficient, it is repetitious. That doesn't matter. What matters is that we reflect on the positive achievements of the day, and share these with the group as a whole. "Camper reports" is an expression of respect for individuals, and respect for the moments that we share. — Dan Mason, director 1977

and start the motor, and then try to fix the motor, and then maybe switch motors, and find a fishing spot and bait hooks and duck hooks and bait more hooks and then try to get back in time for lunch with three tiny blue gills, sacrificed to the joy of the campers." – 1977 Report

All Were Included

The report's details also included Lamb Chop, the goat, that mainly liked to eat leaves and try to get into buildings, and the week that the children from Vasa Children's Home decided a wiener roast for breakfast sounded like fun. It notes a time when the camp's waterfront director, a talented mime, "gave wonderful performances which climaxed with everyone eagerly becoming mimes for a moment, climbing invisible walls and being tugged by unseen balloons. It was an especially fine moment for the deaf campers, who saw him making an exciting communication that included them."

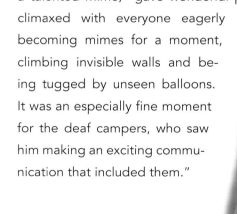

A group of campers embark on a fishing trip on the camp's notorious red pontoon.

The Pontoon Ride

"The pontoon boat ride is an institution at Camp Knutson. We have an old heavy red and brown boat, and lots of people can sit on it at once. The best part is that everyone gets a chance to steer. Some skippers squint intently at the horizon, other find it more fun to turn the wheel and chart a haphazard course around the lake.

A variation on the pontoon ride is the fishing trip. It takes great patience and love on the parts of counselors to dig the worms, get the life jackets on and sort out the rods

Showing Off Accomplishments
Mike Muehlbach, Director, 1980-85

Mike Muehlbach first came to work at Camp Knutson because he was, in his words, "a groupie of the art department at Bethany College in Kansas," and learned about the camp from his professor, Dan Mason. Muehlbach remembers clearly one young girl who exclaimed, "Camp Knutson! It's like Christmas, only better, because it lasts a whole week!" Muelbach wrote:

"Christmas is significant to people spiritually, as the birth of the Christ Child; recreationally, in exploring new games, toys and activities; and socially as a time of reunion with family and friends. Camp Knutson's mission encompasses those same elements plus adds therapeutic and educational components as well.

During those years, Our Savior's Lutheran Church in Minneapolis and Christ Lutheran Church in St. Paul sponsored family camps at Knutson to serve developmentally disabled adults, their parents and siblings. It gave these inner city folks a chance to vacation lakeside for a week without ostracism or glaring stares of others. There would be sing-a-longs, cookouts, and overnight camping, culminating in the end-of-the-week's talent show with Patty's baton twirling and 'high toss' and Anda accompanying herself on the piano singing 'On Top of Old Smokey.'

A group of campers from the Faribault School for the Blind one morning headed to the beach for a water ski lesson...feeling the length of the boat, hands on the propeller, having an almost physics lesson and dry land "practice" on what would pull them up out of the water and onto their skis. Oh to see their smiles!

Left page: Staff play. Above: Waterfront staff water skiing at end of day.

Above: Boys enjoy a trip in camp's original rowboat. Center: Mowing is a regular maintenance job.

Bremwood of Waverly, Iowa, a residential mental health program for adolescents, not only utilized the camp for recreation but at the beginning of each camp season a select group of twenty-four Bremwood teenagers and thirteen staff also made the 350-mile trip to open the camp. As part of Bremwood's work-therapy program, the youth earned money while learning and practicing work-related skills. They brought with them all equipment and supplies, including large Gravely lawn mowers the youth learned to maintain and repair. Those thirty-seven people handled every aspect of preparing the camp—cleaning and painting buildings, clearing grounds, installing docks, restoring outdoor furniture, planting flowers, and constructing hay-bale targets for the archery range. Their special reward was a canoe trip down Daggett Creek culminating in a visit to the Dairy Queen in Crosslake. Later

in the summer, many of these same teens returned for their week of sailing, fishing, ceramics, and showing off their accomplishments to their friends, saying, 'I painted those sills.'

Crosslake Lutheran Church volunteers babysat for the children of the Young Moms and Teen Moms groups so they might attend group meetings on nutrition, setting up babysitting co-ops, and other issues affecting them. These campers were able to return to their lives well rested and with new knowledge and tools to face their

challenges and provide a better life for themselves and their families."

Muehlbach concluded that whether utilized as a resort, a therapeutic experience, a retreat, or a place to expand one's horizons, Camp Knutson enabled the children, adults, and families to be themselves—and to grow, explore, and succeed in a safe environment.

Prince of Glory family camp, with Pastor Mark Hanson (former ELCA Presiding Bishop).

Changing Times

Changing Times and Opening Doors

In its earliest years, Camp Knutson served children and adults with developmental disabilities and those who were identified as "deaf, blind, or emotionally disturbed." Many lived in large institutions. By the late 1960s, people questioned if such institutions could provide nurturing and growth-producing care. Movements began that established more individualized and smaller home settings and programs. Over time, group home residents were given greater choice in how they could spend their money, including their recreational dollars. Smaller groups and fewer people were attending Camp Knutson.

In 1980, the American Lutheran Church turned ownership of Camp Knutson over to Lutheran Social Service of Minnesota (LSS). Proposals had been sought from groups interested in owning the camp. At the time, LSS was the primary user of Camp Knutson for people living with physical and mental disabilities. Likewise, the values LSS as an organization displayed—treating all with dignity

and respect—was well aligned with Knutson's original vision. At the time of the transfer, Camp Knutson required an annual subsidy of close to $30,000.

Left: Entrance to Camp Knutson during the fall. Above: Campers in team-building activity.

Fewer Campers
JoAnn Donner, Director, 1986-87

Quilt auctions became a mainstay to raise funds for camp.

In 1986, JoAnn Donner was hired as Camp Knutson's next director. Donner had a degree in recreation with a concentration in therapy and had worked at Camp Confidence and an LSS group home, both in Brainerd. Prior to her appointment, camper fees had been raised while more communities were offering free recreation programs for people with disabilities, and, according to Donner, even

fluctuating gas prices affected the camp's attendance numbers. Fewer campers were returning.

Camp Knutson's aging buildings were also creating challenges. With many smaller groups now attending camp simultaneously, both campers and staff were living closely with people who were strangers. For Camp Knutson's special needs campers, it was a growing source of discomfort. Camp staff and the advisory council began a more formalized study of the camp and its future.

During this time, an unexpected financial boost came from beyond the camp. Donner had heard of a successful quilt auction fundraiser in southern Minnesota and contacted several quilters at Crosslake Lutheran Church. Would they be willing to take on such a project on behalf of Camp Knutson? The Crosslake women were members of the Paul Bunyon Regional Auxiliary of LSS and the auxiliary quickly agreed. LSS greatly increased the success of the auction by contacting Lutheran churches throughout the Twin Cities and asking for donated handmade quilts.

In 1987, 274 quilts were auctioned, raising $5,000 for the camp. The following year, with the addition of skilled auctioneer Harvey Buchite and matching funds, 276 auctioned quilts raised $14,000 for the camp. For many years, the annual quilt auction was the camp's single largest outside source of support. This enjoyable social event brought people into camp, provided income, and formed a community of supporters. What began as an experiment became a mainstay in Camp Knutson's life.

Strategic Planning
Rob Larson, Director, 1988–95; 1998–present

Rob Larson came on as camp director with an MA in recreational administration from the University of Wisconsin-LaCrosse and experience as a survival skills counselor with Wilder Foundation's St. Croix Camps. By the summer of 1988, many of Camp Knutson's campers were adults. During this time of fluctuating camp attendees, the camp's regular groups offered a financial base and much-welcomed reconnecting between campers and returning staffers who had begun to feel like family.

For Larson and his advisory council, the late 1980s became a time of intense strategic planning, in which they examined every aspect of the camp with an eye to its

CAMP KNUTSON
CAMP KNUTSON UPDATE • SPRING 1988
Rob Larson, Director

Greetings! As the new director of Camp Knutson it is my pleasure to be part of Lutheran Social Service of Minnesota and to have the opportunity to continue the mission of Camp Knutson.

The past few years I have worked with behavior-problem adolescents and emotionally disturbed children. It is my intent to use this experience to provide a quality camping program and to carry on the primary goals of Camp Knutson: to help disabled children and adults feel good about themselves, to respect the dignity of the individual, and to provide an environment for fun and relaxation.

May 7 & 8: Spring Clean-Up Days: Anyone who would enjoy a day at camp to help clean and get ready for summer is most welcome. Make it a family event. Overnight accommodations are available.

May 13, 14, 15: Fishing for Fun: Opening of fishing season at Camp Knutson. You are welcome to come join us for a weekend of fishing. A fee of $25 will include food and lodging, boats, and some gear. If interested, contact Rob Larson by May 1.

future. A study of the adequacy of the camp's buildings noted that the uninsulated Hilltop Cabin, Harold Knutson's former summer home, housed the camp director and his family, the camp office, and the only washer and

Despite deep concerns about the future of camping, letters, such as these examples from two inner-city young mothers, reinforced the camp's mission:

> I am a teen mom who attended camp this year. It was the first time my daughter and I had seen woods and forests. It is a summer I will never forget. I had never been swimming in a lake, had a boat ride, or watched birds paddling on the water. I loved it! It was beautiful and I'll remember it for the rest of my life.

> It was so nice to get the kids away from the city... to feel safe, to be with people I could trust. Being at Camp Knutson showed me what life could be like... and what I want to work towards.

Responding to Risk: *Opening Doors, Creating New Camps, and Community Involvement*

The woods and wildlife were something many campers from the city had never seen.

dryer in camp. The Larsons lived in Hilltop from April to mid-October each year and rented housing in the Brainerd area during the winter months. Advisory council minutes from August 1989 note that "the issue of where the Camp Director lives was discussed. It was noted that for Rob and Beth Larson, having to move their household twice a year was very stressful."

Twice in Camp Knutson's history, in 1991 and 1998, financial pressures placed the camp at risk of being sold. By 1991, camper numbers were continuing to decline, camp buildings were inadequate, and the camp needed an ever-increasing subsidy from LSS. At the same time, LSS was facing pressing social service needs throughout the state while having fewer available funds with which to work.

When Kate Williams, at that time a camp neighbor, read in the *Lake Country Echo* that the camp might be sold, she was concerned. "As a biology teacher for twenty years, I knew that wildlife needed contiguous acres of land to thrive, not just a patch of wilderness here and there. What would a string of pink condos and boat slips do to the thirty acres of Camp Knutson's property and to the surrounding forest and lake ecology?" Williams asked.

Not long after, Williams and her husband, Tom, met with LSS President Mark Peterson and Eleanor Goodall, an LSS Development Director, asking for time to mobilize support for the camp. Williams recalls, "Mark explained in detail the concerns about the camp's financial picture. It was clear he supported Camp Knutson's program, but he also said many people had studied the issues and what we were facing would not be a cakewalk." During that meeting, Peterson arranged for Goodall to assist the group, and she became an immediate help.

Dan Mason, a former director of Camp Knutson and head of its advisory council, spearheaded a group that included the Williamses, Goodall, neighbors Lyle and Tina Joyce, and other friends on the peninsula. They put together a two-pronged campaign to raise awareness of and money

Mason and Eleanor and Bill Goodall at informational Open House.

for the camp and to increase the use of the camp. The three-year CAMPaign for Kids was started with their contributions and leadership and a plan was put in motion to start opening the doors to camp. "Neighbors had an affection for the kids," Goodall said, "from seeing them on the waterfront and at the Dairy Queen. But a lot of neighbors and community really didn't know what went on at camp and the difference camp made in kids' lives. We made immediate plans to change that."

The Joyces opened their home to informational sessions about the camp, the kids it served, and its financial dilemma. The sessions often ended with walks through camp.

Children with hearing impairments learn sign language on the beach and practice while on a trail excursion.

Letters were sent to raise awareness of the very real possibility that the camp might not open the following summer. People hosted bridge parties and dinner parties to raise awareness and money, and camp director Rob Larson and Goodall spoke at area clubs, organizations, and resorts. A growing base of interest and support began to develop. Once the process of raising local awareness was underway, the advisory council set out to secure greater use of the camp.

Creating Camps

Alice LaBarre was a Camp Knutson advisory council member during the efforts to increase the camp's attendance. In her position as Assistant Director of Deaf and Hard of Hearing Services at the Minnesota Deptartment of Hu-

man Services, Alice proposed creating a family camp that would increase communication within families with children living with deafness. As a teen, Alice had come to Camp Knutson for four summers when her parents, Pastor Sterling and Esther Simonson, brought hearing- and vision-impaired children to camp with the Ephphatha Chaplaincy Services. She had seen how Camp Knutson had changed lives.

In 1991, LaBarre worked with Larson to create a one-week camp session for children with hearing impairments and their families—the first of its kind in Minnesota. The camp's classes in American Sign Language (ASL) gave family members a start in communicating with one another. It was at Camp Knutson that many parents saw their children communicating with signing peers and friends for the first time. After camp, one mother wrote: "Camp Knutson provided one of the most profound experiences I've had since our child was born deaf. It was thought-provoking and encouraging. It expanded our vision for what can be." A sibling said, "Now I can tell my brother things. We always liked each other, but it was hard to talk to him before."

LaBarre encouraged staff who were deaf to bring their families as unofficial role models. Parents attended structured lessons but also meals, walks, and conversations with the best experts in Minnesota on hearing loss. Each day started with families telling stories in ASL. Morning and evening ASL classes, activities for the children, family time, and panel discussions rounded out the day. Parents were shown the newest tools and technologies available to help improve communication.

"Families wanted to return again and again to experience the support and to have their children play where there was no communication barrier," LaBarre said. "As a government employee and leader of a division, I felt it was the very best money the state spent."

Carlos's Flying Elephant

When the American Academy of Dermatology brought children to Camp Knutson for the first time in 1993, it became the first camp in the world to serve children with severe skin disorders. It also laid the foundation for Camp Knutson to serve other children who were medically fragile.

Carlos was one of the camp's international campers. He came alone to Camp Knutson from Portugal at age seventeen. Carlos lived with epidermolysis bullosa (EB), a rare disease with chronic, painful blistering inside and outside his body. At the Minneapolis–Saint Paul airport, Carlos saw for the first time in his life several children, including girls, who had his disease. It had never occurred to Carlos that girls might have EB, too.

When the children left for camp, a driver raised Carlos by elevator into the bus. Carlos had lost his feet because of EB and his fingers were bandaged stubs. He commonly repositioned himself by maneuvering with his upper body. When a physician offered to lift Carlos onto the bus seat, Carlos replied softly, but firmly, "No. Just believe in me," and then transferred on his own.

Near the end of the camp week, the children made drawings of what being at camp meant for them. Carlos happily drew himself, asleep in bed smiling, his body wrapped head-to-toe in bandages. In a dream-balloon over his head, Carlos stood with a girl, also covered with bandages. They were smiling together under a rainbow. The following year, Carlos's artwork was a picture of an elephant with wings. "At home I am like an elephant. It is impossible to get around," he said. "At Camp Knutson I can go everywhere. I am an elephant that flies."

Carlos with self-portrait he stenciled with a smiling face.

Additional work by the advisory council in 1991 nearly doubled the number of campers anticipated for 1992. Mark Dahl, a dermatologist, and his wife, Arlene, had a cabin on Whitefish Lake and were part of the support and strategizing for Camp Knutson's future. In Camp Knutson, Dahl saw the possibility of fulfilling a personal, long-held dream. As President of the American Academy of Dermatology (AAD), Dahl proposed to organize a camp session that would allow children with chronic skin conditions to spend a week at camp—in recreation and in making new friends, instead of focusing on their diseases.

During those first years of opening doors to greater possibilities for Camp Knutson, Crosslake's churches sponsored a Camp Knutson informational tea party. In 1994, Immaculate Heart Catholic Church, Crosslake Evangelical Free Church, and Crosslake Lutheran Church sponsored Camp Knutson Sunday. Camp volunteers spoke at the churches' worship services and a special collection was taken.

That same year, Pastor Dick Erickson of Crosslake Lutheran Church and Father Paul Fruth of Immaculate Heart Catholic Church came together to serve on the camp's advisory council. "Supporting Camp Knutson became an ecumenical effort," Fruth said. According to Erickson, a growing commitment to Camp Knutson transcended many barriers often found in small communities.

1994 Community Involvement

The Camp Knutson advisory council hosted a community-wide 4th of July Big Bang celebration for individuals and families, which was enjoyed by more than 100 attendees.

Vacationland Lutheran Brotherhood Branch purchased and built a new boardwalk for the beach.

A new wooden swing was donated to camp in memory of Reverend Sterling Simonson.

Several service organizations—the VFW in Jenkins; American Legions in Pequot Lakes, Pine River, Crosslake, Backus, and Hackensack; and the Lutheran Brotherhood in Brainerd—pooled their resources to buy the camp a new convection oven.

Master Architectural Plan
Rob Lane, Director, 1996~99

It was winter when camp director Rob Lane first toured the camp.

Late in 1995, Rob Larson left Camp Knutson to become director of the Crosslake Community Center, and Rob Lane was hired to fill the position. Lane lived in Nisswa at the time and knew of the camp through his church. Describing his first tour of Camp Knutson in mid-March of 1996, Lane said, "I parked on the main road and forced my way through large snow drifts, while freezing winds blew off the lake. But even with thoughts of, 'What did I get myself into?' I could still imagine what the amazing property would look like when filled with campers."

During Lane's first summer, Camp Knutson hosted Camp Benedict for the first time, bringing together individuals and families affected by HIV/AIDS. Soon after, he received a letter:

We wanted to thank you and your staff for the wonderful experience you provided to our daughter and granddaughter. Prior to coming to camp, our granddaughter would not speak to her mother. She was so mad and sad that her mom had this stigma-filled disease that she completely shut her out of her life. Throughout the week at camp our granddaughter met other teens who were dealing with their parents being HIV positive and by sharing time together she came to realize that just because a bad thing has happened to her mom, it didn't mean her mom was bad. By the end of the week, they were talking again, and when our daughter passed away this fall our granddaughter was there to support her. This would not have been possible without their time at Camp Knutson.

During 1996, Lane oversaw the creation of a master architectural plan, including bids for rebuilding the camp with the assistance of Steve Edwins of SMSQ Architects of Northfield. In 1997, Mark Peterson appointed Bob York, LSS Vice President of Home and Community Living, to work with Lane to help move the improvement of Camp Knutson properties forward. "I knew Bob would be a real asset and an effective voice for the camp with the LSS Board," Peterson said.

As part of long-range planning, Rob Larson returned to camp in July 1998 as operations director, and in the fall, Lane moved to the LSS office in St. Paul to continue building a base of camping partnerships and donors. Before leaving in 2000, Lane made initial contacts with the Autism Society of Minnesota and the Down Syndrome Foundation, who would both later become partnering camps.

In September 1998, discussion about the possible selling of Camp Knutson surfaced once again. By then, camper numbers had increased and mostly stabilized and the camp was self-sustaining, but it lacked the $2.75 million in resources to make improvements that the co-directors and advisory council had presented as essential. For several months, an LSS task force conducted a detailed study to determine if Camp Knutson should be relocated, sold, or improved.

Dick Erickson and Dan Mason coordinated the efforts of those who were determined to keep the camp program and its original land intact. Countless phone calls, group meetings, and one-on-one conversations ensued. Documents were drafted and articles appeared in the area's *Lake Country Echo* and the *Minneapolis StarTribune*. Betty Ryan, writing for the *Lake Country Echo*, covered the matter in detailed articles.

Rebuilding for Good

At the height of activity to determine the future of Camp Knutson, it was estimated that close to $3 million would be needed to make the camp safe, handicapped accessible, and equipped to serve medically fragile children and their staff. Late in 1998, Jerry and Sandy Bilski, camp neighbors, indicated their intention to provide substantial financial support to the camp. Soon after, the Bilskis met with Mark Peterson and offered to co-chair a capital fund drive. Their generosity sparked hope that the camp might be saved.

In early January 1999, the LSS board committed to restore and modernize Camp Knutson and welcomed the Bilskis as leaders in the capital campaign. Once the decision was made to retain the property, a dramatic renewal process began. With the Bilskis' commitment, new construction and

Paul Tillquist, Vice President of Development, and Mary Ella Pratte, Director of Major and Planned Giving, joined the *Rebuilding for Good* efforts.

"Sandy and I told the committee the amount needed to be $6 million," Jerry Bilski said. "$3 million for the buildings and grounds, and $3 million to endow the camp."

"It didn't make sense to us," Sandy Bilski said, "to raise only what was needed for the immediate improvements. The camp needed to be viable into the future." By July 1999, the campaign *Rebuilding for Good* was put in motion. "The name '*Rebuilding for Good*' was deliberately

Ground-breaking ceremonies with the Bilskis, camp staff, LSS staff, and family members.

capital campaign planning began at once. The possibility of losing the camp had generated strong commitments of financial support in the camp's local community, from Crosslake Lutheran Church and far beyond. The LSS board, having studied the camp in detail, was likewise able to put its full support behind moving forward; LSS staff members

Rebuilding for Good Campaign Goals:

Make the public aware of Camp Knutson and its mission

Raise $3 million for construction

Raise $3 million for endowment

Complete the campaign in 5 years

Campaign costs not to exceed 1% of goal

chosen," Sandy said, "to show we were rebuilding for a good cause—the changes the camp makes in the lives of these kids—and that we were rebuilding to stay."

The Bilskis were insistent that all givers be thanked equally regardless of the size of their contribution. Naming opportunities were extended to those whose gifts were sufficient to remodel or finance a building or substantially seed the project. A revised endowment campaign—annual giving called *Friends of Camp Knutson*—was established to obtain funds for camping scholarships and to ensure that the camp's buildings and grounds would be kept current to meet the children's emerging needs.

What happened next is variously described as a series of miracles and the result of diligent work. Over a four-year period, more than two thousand people gave their time, talent, and money to support Camp Knutson's renovation and expansion. Steve Peterson, a local contractor, was hired to serve as lead builder, project manager, and coordinator of volunteers working on the project. Building after building was pledged and constructed in honor of various individuals and institutions: in memory of a teen daughter who loved children, to honor a husband's request, in thanksgiving, because of the good done at

Camp Knutson, in appreciation for blessings, after a church was sold, and more. In all, more than $4 million was raised. Fifteen handicapped-accessible building projects, including eleven new buildings, were completed on time and within budget. Landscaping was added that fit the natural surroundings.

"Each time a building was completed," Bilski said, "Camp Knutson was able to expand the camp's programs or increase its usage. As a result of the transformation, Camp Knutson also became available as a retreat center beyond the summer season." During Camp Knutson's rapid rebuilding, the Crosslake Community Charter School was founded and was in need of a facility. Camp director Rob Larson was contacted and the camp temporarily housed the school in its remodeled dining hall and duplex building on weekdays. The charter school operated at Camp Knutson during the 2000–01 school year, and Camp Knutson used the grounds for retreat camps on the weekends.

Also during *Rebuilding for Good*, men and women from Crow Wing County Jail who were serving time for nonviolent offenses worked at camp as part of the *Sentence to Serve* work-release program. "While they were here, they

learned about our campers and were proud to be working for their benefit," Larson said. By the end of the project, *Sentence to Serve* participants had provided many hundreds of hours of labor to the camp's renewal.

Financial support at every level was described as gratifying, including corporate pledges, family trusts, local community commitments, and individual donations large and small. Support ranged from significant pledges to the summer babysitting earnings of a twelve-year-old. As each building in the master plan was completed, a dedication ceremony was held. "There was a true sense of celebration at the completion of each new project," Larson said.

A Weekend of Celebration

When the campaign to rebuild Camp Knutson began in 1999, plans were made to celebrate the completion of the project on August 23, 2003—the 50th anniversary of Camp Knutson's original dedication. The celebration included a Friday evening donor recognition dinner and a Saturday re-dedication. The weekend brought to camp nearly all the previous camp directors, many alumni staff and campers, donors and "a roomful" of volunteers. LSS President and CEO, Mark Peterson, welcomed the group; Jerry Bilski summarized the *Rebuilding for Good* campaign; and Dan Mason, former camp director and active advisory council member, gave an historical overview of the camp. Former directors and campers shared their camp stories. During the event, Bishop Peter Strommen re-dedicated the camp and Reverend Dick Erickson dedicated two recently completed cabins.

Mason received a Volunteer Recognition Award as part of the event. He first worked at Camp Knutson at age sixteen; his father had helped organize the camp's founding, and over the years, five other family members had served on the camp staff. When Mason was asked why the camp had such enduring impact on camp staff and on three generations of his family, he wrote:

I think we all saw the true joy that being at camp gave to the campers. Whatever issue brought them to camp was not of their doing. These kids, individuals, and families, who were and are routinely left out, are at the center at Camp Knutson. It is their place. I think seeing persons with truly difficult lives finding so much pleasure in their week at camp bonded camp staff to the program.

Then there is the place itself, with the dramatic panorama across Whitefish Lake in the upper camp, and lovely Big Trout Lake at the waterfront. I believe place and purpose are one at Camp Knutson—the experience of the campers and staff can't be separated from the site itself.

Our friends have a son who came home from a session at the Down Syndrome Camp proudly talking about his camp, and showing interest in being more independent and capable. Camp Knutson truly changes lives. Being witness to that changes staff; it changed our family members, it changes volunteers. We know without question that we gain so much more than we could give.

Rob Larson, camp director and master of ceremonies for the 50th anniversary event, described the feeling of exultation as people publicly shared reflections about Camp Knutson from the past half-century. "It was a celebration of thanksgiving for everything that had taken place," he said, "and for a bright future of giving many more children an opportunity to experience Camp Knutson."

Past camp directors at 50th anniversary celebration (l-r): Rob Larson, Andy Boe, Ray Runkel, Mike Muehlbach, Dave Sonnichsen, Dan Mason, Gordon Long, and Rob Lane.

Camp Directors

1954 Ray Runkel
1955-1956 Reub Jessop
1957-1960 Mark Ronning (deceased)
1962 Henry Bjorlie (deceased)
1961, 1963-1965 Gordon Long
1966-1967 Andy Boe
1968-1979 Dan Mason
1980-1985 Michael Muehlbach
1986-1987 JoAnn Donner
1988-1995 Rob Larson
1996-1999 Rob Lane
1998-Present Rob Larson

Camp Knutson Today

Camps Today

From the time campers step off the bus to a warm Camp Knutson welcome, they enter a camp designed especially for them. Those who have been at Camp Knutson before arrive brimming with excitement. "It is so fun being with other kids just like me," one girl explained. "My very best friends are here." One teen boy said simply, "I've waited 364 days for this—to be 'back home' at camp."

Kids who are new to Camp Knutson come with some hesitation. For many it's their first time away from home or family and their first time in a place where they will be mostly outdoors. While every first-time camper has an internal list of "what ifs," the special needs of Camp Knutson's campers make their lists longer. Even so, one camper commented, "After I saw about the fifth person with skin that looked like mine, I just relaxed and quit noticing."

Angela Dining Hall is the heart of the camp where camp director Rob Larson first teaches the "Johnny Appleseed" grace before meals.

Newcomers to Camp Knutson quickly learn that Angela Dining Hall is the heart of the camp. It's where everyone eats together, hears announcements, and gets involved in entertainment put together for their delight. It's there that camp director Rob Larson leads the ever-favorite Johnny Appleseed grace before meals. Newcomers learn about "Angela's living room"—the wraparound deck with a sound system for karaoke and the surrounding lawns and basketball court used for daily activities.

New campers also soon learn that from 2:30 to 4:30 pm is the daily all-camp waterfront time at the sugar-sand beach. There they can be on the water fishing, boating, kayaking, canoeing, sailing, tubing, paddle boating, or pontooning. They can also be in the water swimming, playing water volleyball, or simply sitting on the beach, digging in sand, or talking at the water's edge.

The waterfront patio next to the boathouse holds tables for board games, beading projects, and hanging out with friends and counselors. Close by is a basketball hoop, horseshoes, and tetherball. Depending on the wind, Rob

Larson's signature event—the balloon launch—might take place on the waterfront within easy reach of the rescue boat. According to Larson, "every attempt is a success." If the balloon gets caught in the trees or merely moves a few feet, he still declares it a victory.

A short trek through the woods on the Big Trout Lake shoreline leads new campers to the archery range, the low ropes course, a rock hounding site, and the place to learn fire building, outdoor cooking, and knot tying. The upper camp area holds the nature-based activities, geo-caching, organized games, GaGa ball, and the popular water wars. Horseback riding is an off-site activity.

The primary goal of Camp Knutson is to help handicapped people feel good about themselves. Campers are provided a non-threatening environment where they can break out of limiting stereotypes, express their uniqueness, and expand their capabilities without fear of failure or insensitive attention from others. Each individual, whether staff or camper, is accepted and recognized as a person of great value, and allowed to be at the same time helper and helped, teacher and student, care giver and care receiver.

— *Dan Mason, Director*
Staff orientation, 1970s

Before the first camp arrives, Camp Knutson's incoming program staff spends eleven days in a values-based orientation and training. Dignity, respect, compassion, and unconditional acceptance are its foundation. The partnering organizations bringing campers to Camp Knutson come with similar convictions. Their staff and volunteers are people "with a heart for kids."

Camp Knutson's five partnering groups in 2014— the American Academy of Dermatology, the Autism Society of Minnesota, Camp Benedict, Camp Odayin, and the Down Syndrome Foundation—conduct their own registration, have their own camp name, and set their own camper fees, which for the most part are free or nominal.

Camp Little Pine (ages 10–14)
& Camp Big Trout (ages 14–16)
American Academy of Dermatology (AAD)

In 1993, dermatologist Mark Dahl first hosted AAD's camp for children with chronic skin disorders to fulfill a long-held dream and to help bring new life and resources to Camp Knutson. Since then, the AAD campers have had experiences many never thought possible. Because of volunteer dermatologists, nurses, medical students, and AAD-trained counselors, even campers swathed nearly head to toe in bandages are able to have experiences at the waterfront, on the lake, or on horseback. One boy desperately wanted to float on an inner tube. With a counselor grabbing each corner of a blanket, he was gently carried into the lake and lowered onto a tube. He said it was one of the happiest times of his life and that he felt so free.

Some of these campers live with conditions that are painful, disfiguring, and can shorten life expectancy. They never see others with their disease and often feel isolated. Other children have conditions that cause baldness, skin discoloration, or open sores. Camp Knutson

Despite bandages, children with more severe skin disorders are able to enjoy activities on the water.

AAD campers' activities include waterfront, swimming and sailing.

Campers get to do activities they never thought they could, such as float on a tube on the lake.

frees them from stares, questions, and bullying. Having a counselor at camp who has a chronic skin condition is especially empowering. "These kids relate immediately with us," said one counselor. "They ask us so many questions. They see possibilities for themselves they hadn't held before."

The medical staff during camp is on call around the clock for medical care and for care normally provided by parents. Children with epidermolysis bullosa (EB), a severe skin disease causing internal and external blistering, sometimes need up to three or more hours daily to soak off and replace their bandages. During one particularly painful dressing change, Justin, who was an annual camper, said kindly to a new nurse, "I will probably cry when you do this, but it's okay."

"This is the kind of compassion that surfaces at camp," a counselor said. "A child in pain wanting to reassure his nurse. The kids teach all of us—counselors, staff, volunteers, and fellow campers—so much." In addition to bandage changes, nighttime tube feedings must also be set up and dismantled. One doctor said that by serving in the role of both parent and doctor at camp, he gained "a huge respect for the complexity of these children's lives."

All costs, including transportation, are provided by AAD; professional staff volunteer their time. The program has attracted children from throughout the United States and seven other countries. Four spin-off camps for kids with skin disease exist today, all based on the model developed at Camp Knutson, where campers can experience activities they never dreamt could be a part of their lives.

Camp Hand in Hand
Autism Society of Minnesota (AuSM)

The Autism Society of Minnesota (AuSM) was established in 1971 to provide education, advocacy, and support for people affected by autism from birth through retirement. Camp Hand in Hand, founded in 1977, has been held at Camp Knutson since 2000. Each camper is provided an AuSM-trained counselor—often a college student, para-professional, teacher, or service provider—hired through an application process, who engages with the camper one-on-one throughout the day.

Camp Hand in Hand's thirty-five campers are divided into small groups based on age, gender, and interests. According to Camp Hand in Hand director, Wendy McNeil, "Swimming, boat rides, and tubing are by far their favorite activities. Another huge interest is horseback riding, which is generously provided by an anonymous friend of Camp K. Our July 4th celebration is a wonderful combination of a parade, musical instruments, singing, flag raising, and a toned-down, sensory friendly version of a fireworks display." Hand-in-Hand campers follow a daytime schedule laid out for them in detailed pictures. They choose their evening activities from an illustrated choice board.

The July 4th parade includes a wonderful combination of musical instruments, singing and a flag raising ceremony.

"The Crosslake fire department spends one night with Camp Hand in Hand during each of our three one-week sessions at Camp K," McNeil said. "The excitement that fills the air is contagious when the trucks pull in and the hose is turned on. Campers, dressed in firefighter gear, spraying down the house-on-fire prop is a huge photo op. The culminating event is when the firefighters get on top of their truck and spray the ball field filled with campers and staff running through the water dancing, laughing, and smiling. It's one of our favorite nights! We appreciate the kindness and dedication the firefighters give to our campers and Camp K."

Campers enjoy
toned-down, sensory
friendly 4th of July
fireworks, and
horseback trail riding
at a nearby stable.

Camp Benedict

Camp Benedict was one of the country's first retreats for families affected by HIV/AIDS. It was founded in 1996 by Renee Steffen, a nurse in the Brainerd Lakes area. Steffen saw that especially rural families affected by HIV/AIDS needed a safe and confidential place where they could find mutual support, education, and relaxation. Today, the camp is overseen by Connie Statz, who learned firsthand the importance of education to combat fear and the unknown when she was diagnosed HIV positive following a blood transfusion.

Mornings at Camp Benedict are devoted to education; after lunch, adults join the children for camp activities. For Camp Benedict kids, camp is the place where they can find answers to their questions, probe their feelings and fears, and have fun with those who understand their complex challenges.

HIV/AIDS continues to be a difficult disease to talk about and some families come to camp who have not yet discussed their diagnosis, even within the family. A single father looked to the Camp Benedict group for help and support in telling his ten-year-old daughter she was HIV positive.

A mother described her heartbreak and fear when her doctor told her that both she and her two-year-old son were HIV positive. "When the doctor told me," she said, "it broke my

heart." She became afraid to go to sleep, fearing her son might die in the middle of the night. After attending Camp Benedict, her attitude began to change. "I was able to look at the positive things that were in my life and be grateful for them," she said. "When my attitude changed, so did my son's." Eventually, she began going into area high schools as part of a program to inform students about the possible consequences of risky sexual behavior.

"Camperships" to attend Camp Benedict are raised through the Rhino Ride, a two-day bike ride in the Brainerd Lakes area each August. Camp Benedict cyclists lodge at camp at the end of their first day on the ride. The Bazinet Foundation helps underwrite additional costs.

Rhino Ride raises funds for Camp Benedict each August.

Camp Odayin

Sara Meslow lived with a heart arrhythmia in her teens and later needed an implantable defibrillator. After volunteering during the summers at a camp for young heart patients in California, she returned to Minnesota and founded Camp Odayin in 2001, since nothing similar existed in the Midwest ("Odayin" is the Ojibwa word for "heart"). "When I started the camp thirteen years ago," Meslow said, "I was only thinking about providing the experience of camp for these kids. I never dreamt Camp

Children enjoy less strenuous activities outdoors.

Odayin would also become their 'heart family'—their network of support for themselves and their families."

Some of Camp Odayin's kids live with a sense of limited mortality. One camper last year told new friends, "I'm thankful my track coach knew CPR. If he hadn't, I wouldn't be here." Odayin holds a memorial service at camp each year for former campers who have died during the year.

Odayin's volunteer nurses dispense countless pills, staff the camp's health center (that can convert into a mini-intensive care unit in minutes), and attend every camp

activity. Volunteer cardiologists are in the waterfront's rescue boat and on shore. Odayin-trained volunteers serve as counselors. "Our medical staff love to see their patients enjoying life, swimming, and laughing at camp." Sara said, "And the campers say there's nothing funnier than seeing their cardiologist wrapped in tinfoil for 'time travel' night."

For many of the Odayin campers, this is their first time away from home. Taking part in activities outdoors can be a new and liberating experience. "Our kids are so used to being heart patients, we want this to be a week when

they are just kids," Sara said. "Every camp day ends with our happiness song. We really want our kids to know that life can be happy, that they can choose to be happy," Sara said.

Camp Knutson adjusts for the needs of Odayin campers by scheduling more relay-based or group activities that minimize running, by setting up the geocaching course on more level ground, and by finding ways for those with greater physical limitations to participate, for instance by keeping score or blowing signal whistles. Medical staff recommend last-minute adaptations, if needed.

On their application for camp, returning campers are asked to fill in this prompt: "Because of Camp Odayin..." Joe, an Odayin camper who passed away in January 2014, wrote on his application: "Because of Camp Odayin, I am a better person."

Down Syndrome Camp
Down Syndrome Foundation

The Down Syndrome Camp was created by governing committees of parents and educators who wanted to provide exceptional experiences for young people with Down syndrome.

Angie Kniss, president of the foundation's board of directors, described Camp Knutson as "perfect for our kids. It's safe and welcoming, and it builds their independence and their ability to socialize and cooperate." Kniss said Camp Knutson is where the kids with Down syndrome form their pool of friends. "My son has gone to camp for a number of years. He's a senior in high school and the only one with Down syndrome in his class of 850. When he wants to go bowling, he's not going to call a kid on the football team. He'll call one of his Knutson buddies, and he does that a lot."

"The Down Syndrome Camp is our older kids' spring break trip," Kniss said. "Campers are given small gifts throughout the week to remind them they are special, and we take trips to a local bowling alley and to a horse stable." For many of the campers, childhood milestones happen at Camp Knutson: the first time away from home, the first time sleeping in a bunk, the first time on a horse, the first dance, the first time being surrounded by others who share their experience, the first time of playful teasing and flirting. "I wish you could see the looks on their faces," Kniss said. "You can just see their spirits fly."

The Down Syndrome Foundation supports the camp through scholarships; by underwriting basic costs, including materials, equipment, and camper supplies; and by providing stipends for staff.

Campers enjoy dancing on the beach, horseback riding, fishing and other outdoor activities.

Minneapolis Community Group

Adults living with persistent mental challenges have attended Camp Knutson since the mid-1950s. For the last session of the 2014 season, Camp Knutson will host the Minneapolis Community Group (MCG), an adult mental-health aftercare group that also includes members with developmental disabilities. Some of the campers who will attend this summer have done so every summer since 1968, when LSS group social worker Allan Bostelmann first arranged for MCG to attend camp. The group made their first trip to camp in a rented school bus with a picnic lunch stop along the way, which became tradition. Many of the group's members had lived for years in highly regimented state hospitals. For them, choosing camp activities in which to participate was particularly stressful.

With gentle guidance from camp staff, some of the campers became more comfortable making decisions and began to develop life-changing skills.

Staff and campers shared activities, did "KP" (Kitchen Patrol) together, sang around the campfire, and slept in the same building. "That atmosphere, plus being out in nature, seemed to bring out the best in people," Bostelmann said. "Members lost their self consciousness. They laughed, tried things out, and had fun. Many went to surrounding towns for sightseeing and souvenirs. By the end of the week, most of them wanted to participate in what became the world's longest talent show."

One woman recently said she feels close to God in such a lovely setting. "At camp I wrote my first of many songs

and learned to take my songwriting seriously," she said. One member, who has attended camp each summer for twenty-six years, said his barber gives him free haircuts so he could put that money in a camp account. "When Hennepin County cut their support for camping programs in 2007, I wrote letters, circulated a petition, and appeared before the county board," the MCG member said. "Among other things, I told them that looking forward to camp and having the benefit of it once a year kept people taking their medication and out of regional treatment centers and psychiatric units." Hennepin County restored $75,000 to camping programs that year.

Camp Knutson Staff

In 2000, Kate Williams, a former high school and college teacher, joined Camp Knutson as assistant director, responsible for all aspects of the summer program. Since then, Williams has spent each January and February building the camp's staff of fifteen, pouring over applications and interviewing from a broad pool of candidates. In order to assure the best blend of staff, counselors wishing to return again as staff are asked to reapply.

In orientation and training, staff is introduced to the key people and places at camp and learns the importance of the daily schedule which can change each week depending on the needs of the campers. Together staff prepare curriculum and learn to demonstrate and teach all camp activities. They also create the programming that will determine the themes, skits, supporting costumes, and props they weave throughout the camp day. Foremost in their orientation is learning the needs of the special populations Camp Knutson serves. Williams often asks Caroline and Dan Mason, former camp staff, to talk about the camp's history, its philosophy of service, and their experiences with the campers. Experienced staff join in and share camper stories. One story remembered by Dan

Mason, about a youth we will call Keith, took place at the airport on departure day:

The kids were stumbling off the bus from camp, disheveled and deeply tired. They had not slept much the night before and they were sober at the prospect of saying goodbye to new friends.

Keith, who lives with EB, had five exhilarating days swimming, boating, riding horseback, making arts and crafts projects, singing in the dining hall and around the camp-

Above center: Sharing a fascination with "goop." Above right: Kate Williams demonstrates making "hamberjoes."

as campers say goodbye to their friends, but this was different. Keith's sobs were wracking, from a place of profound sorrow deep within. Immediately, the gathering grew silent and several boys raced to his wheelchair and stood with him, touching him, talking to him quietly as he regained control. His friends seemed to understand where his grief came from, and stood by him—a remarkable thing for 12-year-old boys to do.

Mason describes this scene "as the miracle of camp—that Keith has a painful, disfiguring disease for which there is no cure, but Camp Knutson gave him the chance to act like a regular kid and make wonderful friends who understand the challenges he lives with each day." During their orientation, staff also discuss the impact that multiple surgeries or continuous pain can have on kids, and what staff might be do to empower campers so their health conditions don't become the way they define themselves.

Staff make the camp experience special for the campers.

fire, and enjoying the talent show, carnival, and dance. Best of all, he had made real friends with kids who share his life situation.

The scene at the airport is a noisy chaos of campers, staff, and escort volunteers. Only once over the years has the group grown silent and it was the day when Keith began to cry. Tears are a main feature of departure days,

Second-Level Learning

During orientation, Williams discusses second-level learning, that no matter what staff are teaching—archery, a new game, canoeing, a rope ladder—a second level of learning is going on. At that deeper level, campers trying new things are learning about being a friend, giving support, asking for help, and being excited trying something new. Patience is learned while they wait their turn. Through all the activities, campers are learning that Camp Knutson is a place where they will be loved and cared for and where they will be safe and have fun.

Staff discuss how they might engage a particular child and how they might plan so that campers can succeed in what they are trying. They consider what they want to teach, how they are going to do it, and how they can adjust if they need to. In orientation, time is set aside for "deep listening," one-on-one sharing without interruption that builds deep respect and appreciation for one another.

Throughout the summer, staff regularly debrief and share with one another the impact that campers are having on their lives. Asked if they would share their stories with *Where Spirits Fly*, Becca, a repeat staff member and for-

Campers learn about working together as teams with a plank walk.

mer coordinator wrote, "My summers at Camp Knutson were the most exhausting and rewarding summers of my life. The joy, strength, and inspiration we got from the campers was the energy that motivated our staff. We survived every late night of planning, unclogging toilets, and working fund-raisers by saying 'it's for the kids.'"

Robalee described being engulfed in a culture of compassion and acceptance at camp she had never known. "Soon after getting to camp," she said, "I realized that, regardless of the countless places we come from, each of us craves a smiling face, a listening ear, and a person to recognize our potential."

Above left: Staff take a camper on his "first-time-ever" tubing ride. Above right: Staff dress country as they introduce campers to animals they may have never seen.

Marie wrote that a camper living with blindness taught her a lesson about capabilities. "We were at the rope wall on the camp's trust course when I first asked the camper if she wanted a turn climbing the wall. 'Not yet, thanks,' was the answer." Later in the week, wrapped in the cheers of the other campers and staff, the camper grabbed onto the rope wall and took one step upward. Totally triumphant, smiling ear-to-ear with accomplishment, the camper returned to the ground. "I learned instantly what camp emphasizes," Marie wrote, "that every victory is to be equally celebrated, whether a camper scales the entire rope wall in under three seconds or touches the ropes for the first time; that we are brought together to build each other up for our successes, not tear each other down for our perceived failures; and that we must never assume we know the capabilities of others."

Eric wrote of being inspired daily by the optimism and courage of the campers, despite the challenges they face: the Camp Odayin youth who proudly display their scars during waterfront, the campers with Down syndrome who always offer smiles and words of comfort to those in need, and the several campers with autism who happily insist on helping with meal clean-up. "They are the building blocks that make our camp community so strong and supportive," Eric said, "and I am forever grateful for the ways in which they so selflessly touched my life."

In describing the impact the campers have had on their lives, summer staff say that working with the camp directors, Rob Larson and Kate Williams, is also life-changing. "Kate is the welcoming, enthusiastic face that brings us together. Her activities begin lifelong friendships," one staffer wrote. Many say Kate is the glue that holds camp together. "Kate provides a positive, caring, and open work environment. We work hard, but we laugh a lot and have fun," one staffer wrote. "She sets the tone for the positive, loving, and fun environment at camp."

Many wrote about Kate's compassion, how carefully she listens, and her ability to help bring out the best in others. "She taught us how to best work with each other to maximize our different strengths," one counselor wrote. "When I get down on myself, I remember Kate saying, 'No matter who you are or what you've done, you can continue to bring happiness and purpose to others.'"

Staff say Rob is "a calm but powerful presence, the director of the camp but also its host, who works to cultivate a loving, accepting and safe environment for each and every camper, counselor, and staff member." They describe Rob as holding everyone accountable to their role to keep camp working smoothly, but in the most sincere

and caring ways possible. One staff member wrote, "Rob taught me to work my hardest, but grant myself forgiveness if something goes wrong. The way he understands struggles and mistakes and encourages growth, fosters trust in his staff." Another said, "Rob knows when our staff is stressed and finds fun ways to provide relief, or he just cleans the kitchen to take one item off our list."

"Rob taught us to not get so caught up in the details that we miss the big picture," a staffer said. "He said the beauty of things is found when we take a step back and realize that even if things don't go perfectly each and every day, we're all still having fun and our camp is everything our kids hope it to be."

A staff member congratulates a camper who found her way through the string maze.

The Work of Many

The volunteer and staff dedication to Camp Knutson can be seen as soon as one comes down the driveway into camp. The camp's buildings and grounds are uniformly beautiful, simple, and well cared for. They reflect the respect that the staff, campers, and volunteers have for nature and the camp's facilities. Flowerbeds are scattered around the grounds. Strict guidelines about keeping "everything in its place" keep the property free of the clutter of toys, games, and equipment. Ask camp director Rob Larson what makes Camp Knutson work the way it does and you will hear what he says over and over again: "It's the community's involvement that has made the biggest difference." The hands-on effort of countless volunteers, near and far, keeps Camp Knutson vital.

Camp Knutson Volunteers (CKV)

Volunteers from CKV read to campers, host "tailgate" dinners and take them fishing.

Many of the volunteers living nearby are members of the organization Camp Knutson Volunteers (CKV). In 2001, Joan Thayer pulled together approximately fifteen women in the Crosslake area who were volunteers and wanted to meet new people. On Joan's front porch, they explored the idea of becoming an organized group that would have fun while they served their community. Camp Knutson became the focus of their efforts.

In 2003, CKV hosted an upscale sale they called a "cabin sale," and a well-attended community-wide luncheon at the Antlers restaurant at Breezy Point. They persuaded local card groups and exercise classes to charge nominal fees to be donated to Camp Knutson. In 2004, the group hosted its first Night Under the Stars and a popular tea party held under white tents in the Crosslake Town Square, complete with hats and white gloves. The volunteers also took on the task of readying the camper cabins each weekend for the incoming campers.

By 2011, the active volunteers numbered more than 100, and CKV developed bylaws and defined their mission. Today they are committed to making a difference in the camping experience of each Camp Knutson child by assisting with camper activites, helping maintain the camp's grounds and facilities, and organizing fundraising events. Those who pay nominal dues are eligible to hold office and vote on matters impacting the camp volunteers. One volunteer who works on fundraising events said, "The camp's work with kids is an unbelievable cause that is deeply values-based. You can feel it in the atmosphere at camp. I volunteer to work on fundraisers because of the camp's values and because I like that we know exactly what we're working toward. An item is chosen off the

camp's wish list—a van, dock sections, or 'camperships,' for example—and we work specifically for it."

Since 2004, Gail Peterson has coordinated and scheduled the volunteers needed by the program staff to offer specific help, such as reading, telling stories, and playing games with specific children; helping with crafts, canoeing, fishing, and biking; hosting a "tailgate dinner"; or baking. In the spring, the volunteers plant gardens and divide perrenials and continue to weed and water weekly throughout the summer. Whether interacting with campers, cleaning cabins, or participating in fundraisers, the

CKV members consider all the work they do to be of equal importance to the vitality of the camp.

Couples who have helped host the camp's "tailgate dinners" say that the casual events support the kids in getting to know each other and form friendships. "It's fun talking with them and seeing them hanging around in groups, laughing and talking," a volunteer said. "The kids love having their hamburgers and bratwurst cooked outdoors and the food served from the back end of our trucks or hatchbacks. Many of them have never seen such a thing. They are so appreciative. You go home just feeling good about the whole thing."

Campers make beaded items that are sold in a local gift shop, with the proceeds going back to the camp.

In 2004, volunteer Kathy Morgan set up a beading and jewelry-making program that brings together volunteers and the summer campers with chronic skin diseases and heart diseases. "I heard about Camp Knutson in my exercise class," Morgan said, "and went to their Night Under the Stars event to learn more." Morgan discovered that her former high school biology teacher, Kate Williams, was the camp's assistant director and by evening's end, Morgan committed to teach a beading class at camp. Once held in the craft center, the beading program now takes place at the waterfront on the boathouse patio.

"The kids love working where all the action is." Morgan said. "More boys join us now."

In the beginning, the campers made bracelets and keychains. "Some of the kids were without fingers, but they wouldn't let us help them," Morgan said. "When they did ask for help, they were so appreciative." Now, rings, bracelets, lizards, and spiders have all been favorite projects. Larger beads are used in making letter openers, bottle openers, and designer forks and spoons. "The kids do very nice work and they are truly proud of what they produce," a volunteer said. "They are surprised when they see the quality of Kathy's supplies. They say, 'Oh my gosh, I would buy this. It's so beautiful.'" Morgan teaches new projects each year. "I always do a test run with a group of young people during the winter," Morgan said, "and I choose only projects I know the campers can succeed at."

The campers' one-of-a-kind pieces go home with them and extras are made to sell at camp events. Lakes Area Gallery and Frame Shoppe in Crosslake also sell the beadwork, with all the proceeds returning to the camp. The beading program now draws on a core group of twenty volunteers, trained and scheduled by Morgan, who work with an average of 750 campers througout the summer and extended retreat season.

A Broad Spectrum and Long Legacy of Volunteers

Volunteers have a long legacy at Camp Knutson; some say their initial connection with camp even changed their life. Dan Thorson, former waterfront staff for three years beginning in 1970 and longtime camp volunteer and benefactor, actively pursued his lifeguard job at Camp Knutson while he was in college. "The experience totally changed my life," Thorson said. "My family had always believed in giving service, but coming to camp put me together with groups of people I had never been exposed to before. The campers taught me what it means to be compassionate and grateful. They opened my heart to give and to share and to help others."

Thorson went from being a business administration major to going into specialized education, obtaining a master's degree in deaf education, and working with emotionally disturbed youth. He later entered the business world, which eventually enabled him to maintain an active life of philanthropy that he describes as a true joy. Thorson has served on the Lutheran Social Service board for a number of years and each September has arranged for groups from his church to work at Camp Knutson with adult campers living with mental health challenges. Thorson's wife, Sandi, is an active partner in volunteering and philanthropy. "I have always thrived on getting people involved in causes," Thorson said, "and Camp Knutson is my favorite cause. I've seen people's hearts be opened by their connection with Camp Knutson the way mine first was."

Above left: Volunteers power wash buildings on a work weekend. Above right: Members of Pastor Paul's work group refurbish an outhouse.

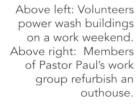

Every spring since 2003, the camp has been readied for the season by approximately fifty employees, family members, and friends of the North American Banking Company (NABC) who come to Camp Knutson for a work weekend. "We're a fun-loving group of serious workers who tackle a lot of work in a short amount of time," one volunteer said. Their tasks include mowing lawns, washing screens and windows, power washing the gables on eleven buildings, splitting wood, and setting up a fountain in the garden. Five people work a full day doing dock-related setup while others repair broken fences and replace any rotting decking around the cabins. Michael

Bilski, President of NABC, serves as resident chef during the work weekend and, while most in the group volunteer out of a passionate commitment to Camp Knutson's work in changing kids' lives, Bilski's meals and the camp's setting are known to be added incentives.

Also in spring, beginning in 1990, Pastor Paul Schaedig has brought Pastor Paul's work group, retired laymen and pastors from Waverly, Iowa, to Camp Knutson for a four-day work trip that occasionally includes fishing. The group has helped cut, split, and stack firewood, paint, make a concrete basketball court and a backstop for the ball field, scrub and reseal the dining room floor, and construct cubicles at the boathouse. In 2007, when they refurbished and restored the outhouse once used by Harold Knutson—for its historical value only—they jokingly said it was their most significant job to date.

During the summer, Crosslake Lutheran Church members help maintain the camp's grounds. The church's participation as active volunteers at Camp Knutson began with women babysitting as far back as 1977; they later made quilts for the auction and pillowcases for the skin disorder camps and helped with occasional spring cleanup. In 1994, when Reverand Dick Erickson became interim pastor at the church, a men's group was formed to do service projects at the camp. Since then, once a month from late spring through mid-fall, up to twenty-five men have breakfast at camp and spend the morning mowing lawns, landscaping, cleaning the dining hall, and doing whatever else is on the director's list. In the early 2000s, when rebuilding began at Camp Knutson, members of Crosslake Lutheran Church said it was their time to "step up to the plate" and pledged the funds and labor necessary to rebuild the camp's former "duplex"—now called Crosslake Lutheran Cabin—and more.

Over the years, volunteer groups have helped keep the camp's activities current. In 2011, members of Zion Lutheran Church in Amor, Minnesota, built a new game court called the Ga Ga pit. The enclosure resembles an animal pen and is used for a gentler version of dodgeball. More than twenty campers can pile into the pit to play, using a jumbo nerf ball. The game's contained space makes it easily adaptable to the campers' physical abilities. Materials for the Ga Ga pit were purchased through a grant from Crow Wing Power and Light.

Crosslake Lutheran Church members work on Crosslake Lutheran Cabin.

Volunteer escorts greet children at the airport.

Since 1993, Dan Mason has recruited and coordinated airport escort volunteers who come to the Minneapolis/St. Paul airport as Camp Knutson's first welcoming presence for children with skin disorders who come from around the nation and the world to spend a week at camp. As they step off the plane, each child is greeted by an escort who stays with them in a welcome area until all the children have arrived and are on the bus to camp. At the end of the camp week, an escort joins each child and stays with the child until his or her departure. It is with the escorts that some children see for the first time others who have their same skin disease. "It is a powerful experience," Mason said. "We also see the children's strength and courage as they navigate the airport concourse seeming not to notice people's stares and double takes as they pass by." Members from Edina Community Lutheran Church have been the core of the escort group over the years. Other volunteers have included faculty, staff, and students from North Hennepin Community College, LSS State Center staff, former Camp Knutson staff, and members of Gloria Dei Lutheran Church in St. Paul. In 2013, the airport volunteer program had a pool of 46 volunteers.

Children who have had or will have heart transplants also head to Camp Knutson from all across the country. These campers are flown into the Brainerd airport on Angel Flights piloted by owners of private planes. Sometimes a pilot flies the same child to camp year after year. Camp Knutson volunteers meet these campers at the airport, take them to camp, and bring them back to the airport at the end of camp. Betsy Simon, a frequent airport volunteer, said, "It's very rewarding to be a volunteer who greets a first-time, nervous camper and then sees their happiness and hears their camp stories and songs at the end of the week. When there are two or more campers in the car, it can be a hilarious sing-along." Six Brainerd-area volunteers are available to meet the flights.

Camp Knutson has had some form of advisory board since its founding in 1953. Fourteen members now serve on the Camp Knutson advisory council. They are a sounding board for the camp's director, offering support, feedback, and direction as they help to plan for the camp's future. Its members often have strong ties with the camp—former camp staff, representatives from its partnering camps, donors, or community members. One member who is a former counselor explained, "Once the camp gets in your blood, it's pretty hard not to stay involved." Their individual work ranges from liaising with the Crosslake planning commission to catering events,

coordinating airport escort volunteers, and speaking on behalf of the camp.

When investment income weakened in the early 2000s, *Friends of Camp Knutson* was formed to provide camper scholarships, or "camperships," and to ensure that the camp buildings and grounds continued to be safe, accessible, attractive and suited to the needs of the campers. Members of the *Friends of Camp Knutson* group—individuals, families, churches, and other organizations—each donate $1,000 or more per year to Camp Knutson. An advisory committee oversees the use of the funds and provides an annual report to *Friends of Camp Knutson* members. Michael and Dennis Bilski co-chair the *Friends of Camp Knutson*. "I'm a *Friend of Camp Knutson*," one woman said, "because I live most of the year in Crosslake. For me, it's part of the commitment that comes with living in a small town. This is the camp's home and the camp does so much good. I give each year so it will stay healthy now and for years to come."

Fund-Raising Events and Celebrations

Night Under the Stars

Camp Knutson Volunteers hosts two events each year to raise awareness about Camp Knutson and to raise funds for specific camp needs. Night Under the Stars, held in July, brings people together for a catered gourmet dinner, silent and live auctions, wine bar, and sale of jewelry made by campers. The event, which in 2013 attracted 300 people, is held at Camp Knutson, where attendees can see the beauty of its grounds and the facilities where campers spend their week. Dinner is served outdoors under two large tents, and the silent auction, which offered more than 200 items in 2013, is located in the dining hall.

Night Under the Stars relies heavily on volunteer help. In 2013, eighty CKV members actively participated on teams set up to manage all aspects of the event, including

Funds raised at the silent auction during Night Under the Stars are used for specific camp needs, like the new van purchased in 2013.

designing invitations, organizing ticket sales and seating, managing publicity, arranging catering and dining facilities, securing auction items, setting up the silent auction, managing attendee registration and check out, and handling parking and cleanup. Night Under the Stars in 2013 raised more than $75,000; a silent donor match of $50,000 raised the total to $125,000. The funds were used to purchase a new van for camper transportation and designated for a much-needed boy's dormitory, to be built in 2014–15.

Taste Luncheon

For those who like a tiny taste of a new recipe before making it, the annual Camp Knutson Taste Luncheon in September is the event to attend. Begun in 2010 by the Camp Knutson Volunteers, the luncheon offers guests a tablespoon-size taste of as many as 34 different recipes as well as a take-home recipe book. Crosslake Lutheran Church graciously provides the use of their kitchen and fellowship hall for the event. Early in the year, recipes are sought from the Camp Knutson Volunteers. A committee of volunteers prepares and tastes each submission, and selects 30–34 recipes for its luncheon guests. On the day of the Taste Luncheon, recipes that can be made in advance are prepared by the person who initially entered the recipe in the competition. Recipes requiring more immediate preparation are put together by a kitchen crew of 8–12 CKV members, in a finely orchestrated sharing of the church's kitchen space and equipment—baking ovens, warming ovens, refrigerators, mixers, counters, and sinks—on a very tight serving schedule. Luncheon guests vote on their favorite recipe in each of four categories: starters, soups and such, salads and sides, and sweets. In 2013, a sold-out group of 225 guests raised approximately $7,000 for "camperships," craft supplies, horseback riding fees, and lifeguard training for counselors.

Camp Knutson Taste Luncheon Recipe Book 2013

The Woods
Landscaping

Ice Tee Open

Two popular fundraisers, spearheaded by groups outside Camp Knutson, involve hundreds of people lending a hand. The Ice Tee Open held at Moonlite Bay Family Restaurant & Bar in Crosslake on the first Saturday in March, was dreamt up in 2001 by owners and staff of the restaurant on a "really boring March day." According to Jesse Eide, one of the owners of Moonlite Bay, "March is just such a slow month in Crosslake. We missed having people around. Lucian Greeninger from Golden Eagle—who lays out the Ice Tee's 18-hole course—knew about a winter golf event in the Twin Cities. What began as a conversation about 'getting a little life in the place' ended as a plan for a Camp Knutson fundraiser."

2014's Ice Tee Open included a silent auction, a costume contest, and a hole-in-one contest, with "hole sponsors" and members of a "500 Club" who individually or jointly pledged $500 to the event. "Each year we keep saying we should be able to raise a little more money and awareness for the camp and everything it does for the kids. This year the weather was against us—a -20° windchill—but the community still came together and raised $21,000," Eide said. "When our distributors come in, I tease them. I tell them they better give me something really good for the silent auction. They laugh. Everybody feels good about doing something for such a good cause right in our own community." Eide added there is nothing that feels better at the end of the day than writing the big check for the camp. "Each year I tell myself I'm not going to get choked up when we present it, and each year we all do. Everyone here cheers; they all love it."

Left: The 18-hole golf course on the lake. Above left: Family enjoys course during Ice Tee Open. Above right: Friends hoping to win the costume contest.

Quilts are auctioned
from the deck of the
dining hall.

Annual Quilt Auction

When the annual Camp Knutson Quilt Auction—usually held the second Saturday in August—is in full swing, the atmosphere is electric. Many in the area plan summer entertaining around the quilt auction, making it a full-day annual event. Exquisite quilts—works of art—are on display in the dining hall. A silent auction showcases smaller handwork items. Artisans from Minnesota and beyond who make and donate objects to the annual Camp Knutson Quilt Auction say the work gives them a special sense of purpose throughout the year. "I think about those kids while I work," one quilter said. "Most of us do. I pray for them and the camp. I think about what many of them have to live with and I get strength from their courage."

In 1987, the Paul Bunyon Regional Auxiliary of LSS began the quilt auction to bring added income to Camp Knutson; in 2013 the auction raised $57,000. For the first ten years, the donated quilts were measured, catalogued, tagged, and stored at the nearby home of Isabel Kunkel. Since 1998, Mission of the Cross Missouri Lutheran Church in Crosslake has received and stored the quilts. Two auctioneers have added to the success of the auction

over the years: Harvey Buchite volunteered his services for the first eighteen years and when he moved away from the area, Glen Fladeboe was hired to take over.

In 2010, the Fund-a-Need option was added to the live auction for people wanting to contribute to Camp Knutson without buying a quilt. Rob Larson identifies a camp wish or need, bidding begins, and the money is raised within minutes. Camp staff members add to the action by digging into the camp's huge costume wardrobe and magically appearing as different characters throughout the afternoon. Bratwurst and hot dogs cooked on the camp's outdoor grill remains part of the auction tradition.

Pancake Breakfast

Each year since 1994, a Camp Knutson Pancake Breakfast has been held on Labor Day weekend to thank neighbors and the community for their involvement. Susann Zeug-Hoese and members of her family were part of that first breakfast for twenty people. Cooking and serving the pancake breakfast is now an established family tradition that includes three generations of the Zeug-Hoese family, with a grandson waiting in the wings to become the fourth. According to Zeug-Hoese, "What began as a Camp Knutson thank you to the neighbors on the peninsula has turned into a huge block party that includes people's Labor Day guests."

In 2013, with the help of additional volunteers, 442 hungry guests were served 1,000 pancakes, bacon, sausages, and fruit in just under two and a half hours.

Three generations of the Zeug-Hoese family serve a pancake breakfast on Labor Day weekend.

A memorial garden honoring Clara Hinkley, founder of the Paul Bunyon Regional Auxiliary, is the sight that greets guests when they enter camp. The metal sculpture, "Changing Lives," is the work of local artist Jeff Kreitz.

CAMP KNUTSON

Today, Camp Knutson has a solid foundation of people dedicated to its mission of changing lives for kids. Thanks to the commitment of so many, the camp's donor base has broadened, the mailing list has grown from 300 households in 1999 to over 3,000 in 2014, and a large group of individuals actively give hands-on service of one form or another. At the same time, new volunteers and supporters are always needed and welcomed. Fresh ideas, experiences, and resources are essential to the camp's potential and ability to serve.

Camp Knutson's profile is that of a premier facility for populations of children with complicated special needs. While the camp has always been known for making life-changing contributions to the lives of those it has served, it is at its strongest now.

Afterword

How the Real World Should Be

When Ally was ten, she came to Camp Knutson during the American Academy of Dermatology's week for kids with skin diseases. She returned for thirteen consecutive years as a camper, volunteer counselor for kids like herself, and finally, a full-time Camp Knutson summer staff. "The opportunity allowed me to realize even more how incredible life is, how blessed we are to have it, and how those special kids have a very important place in this world," Ally wrote. "I could have never guessed that day when I got off the bus how much being at camp would change my life forever. From the little camper I was, to who I am now, I owe it all to Camp Knutson. It has been the most significant thing in my life, and I can't imagine where I would be without it. It has given me the confidence I need to be brave in the world, and it has also taught me to be grateful, compassionate, and happy."

During Ally's last summer on full-time summer staff, she had to leave camp before the final staff celebration and asked that this letter be read in her absence:

For as long as I can remember, I have been different.
Every day I wished to be "normal."
Every birthday candle.
Every four leaf clover.
Every prayer before bedtime.
Every penny in the fountain.
Every star... I made the same exact wish.

I wished and wished, but every day I would wake up the same. I didn't understand why I looked the way I did, and I didn't like it. I was jealous of my peers. I was ashamed of me. And then, I came here. I met other people like me and I met others worse off than I, and in five days, I was changed forever.

The reason I am telling you this is because sometimes I think we don't realize what is happening right in front of our eyes. The simple things we do not think about or pay attention to are life-altering for others. For me, it was people like you. It was people like you who held my hand

without asking what was wrong, without looking at me differently, without fear. It was something foreign to me, and I began to think that maybe if these people didn't think I was weird, maybe I wasn't, after all.

In every diseased person's life there comes a day I call "acceptance day." Acceptance day occurs in one life-defining sentence. It occurs when you are able to say, "I am glad this happened to me. The person I would be without this disease is not as good as the person I am with it."

I can honestly say that without Camp Knutson, the friends I have met here, the people I have come to know, and the acceptance I have learned, I would not have had this day. But I have, and I do, over and over again. And it happens here more than we know. The little things we do allow others to look at themselves in a different light and brings them to their acceptance day.

I just want us all to remember how truly lucky we are. And, I want us to use this insight in our futures. Please, do not forget this camp, these people, or these memories. For some, this may seem like just a job. But it is really so much more than that. We have been blessed to be here. We have learned more than we know. One of the campers said it best last year when he said, "Camp-world is how the real world should be."

The real world should be full of kindness, compassion, love, and acceptance. After all, we all only get one shot at this life thing. It needs to be the best we can make it. So when we all go back to the real world, don't forget this, because what you have been doing here, you can do in that other world, too. You can hold someone's hand without asking what's wrong, without looking at them differently, without fear. It is one of the best gifts you can give.

I love you all. I just wanted to make sure you all know how important this place and you people are to me, and to so many others. You make lives; I hope you know that.

Rebuilding for Good
New or Rebuilt Facilities

The *Rebuilding for Good* campaign, from 1999 to 2003, raised more than $4 million enabling Camp Knutson to expand its facilities to meet the needs of children living with increasing complex challenges. Naming opportunities were extended to those whose gifts were sufficient to build, renovate, or substantially provide for the construction of Camp Knutson facilities. Those gifts were augmented by the donations of more than two thousand people who contributed to the campaign.

Angela Hall

Angela Hall was named in memory of Angela Ritt, the mother of Sandy Bilski, in honor of her devotion and commitment to children. Gifts to rebuild and expand the dining hall were given by Jerry and Sandy Bilski and their extended families, who along with friends also built the dining hall's wrap-around outer deck.

Thorson Boat House and Thorson Bath House

Thorson Boat House provides an upper sleeping area and lower storage for waterfront equipment. Thorson Bath House provides a bathroom, sauna, shower, and changing room. Both were given by Dan and Sandi Thorson in honor of Dan's life-changing experiences as a Camp Knutson lifeguard and counselor during his college years.

Allie's Staff House

Allie's Place was given by Le and Barb Boyer in honor of their granddaughter, Alexa (Allie) Kristine Cusick. Allie is an identical twin whose twin sister died in utero. At that time Allie had a stroke, an event that resulted in severe developmental disabilities and rendered her a quadriplegic. Allie's abilities and disposition have helped those around her, including siblings and friends, learn deeper compassion.

Bazinet Recreation Center

Bazinet Recreation Center features a large recreation area, an arts and crafts room, the canteen, three large storage areas, and a bathroom. It was donated by the Bazinet Foundation and was the first building constructed in the *Rebuilding for Good* campaign.

Crosslake Lutheran Cabin

Crosslake Lutheran Cabin, formerly known as the Duplex Cabin, houses staff from the partnering camps, off-season campers, a laundry, and a meeting area. Funds and 1,000 hours of sweat equity were provided by Crosslake Lutheran Church whose members have had an association with Camp Knutson for more than forty years.

Prince of Glory Hilltop House

Prince of Glory Hilltop House, the original cabin of Harold Knutson, provides staff with office space and housing. Hilltop House was remodeled and winterized with a gift of money from the members of Prince of Glory Slovak Lutheran Church in Minneapolis following the sale of their church.

Husby Family Lodge

The Husby Family Lodge was given by Mary Husby. Mary was inspired by the last wishes of her beloved husband, Joseph, to give a generous gift to Lutheran Social Service to help children. The lodge comfortably accommodates 16 people.

Pauly's Place

Pauly's Place, a welcome center, health services building, and camp office, is dedicated to the memory of Paul Joseph Polaczyk, an eight year-old boy whose inner beauty and loving nature brought healing, peace and joy to all he met. It was erected in the hope that all who visit Camp Knutson will feel the healing power of peace and love.

Renner East and Renner West

The Renner Cabins, two domitories that each provide housing for up to 36 campers, were the gift of Jim and Linda Renner who had a cabin near Camp Knutson for 23 years. Jim and Linda are members of the camp's advisory council and Jim is a former member of the Lutheran Social Service board of directors. Their generosity flowed from their personal mission to help children, especially children with special needs, through a church organization.

Sheena Heath Staff House

Sheena Heath Staff House was named in memory of Sheena Heath, a high school student who dreamed of working with children with special needs. Sheena's parents, David and Carole Heath, believed that the staff house would be a fitting memorial to their daughter and her dream. It comfortably sleeps 9.

Timberlane Lodge

Timberlane was made possible through the generosity of John and Karen Meslow in gratitude for Camp Knutson's work with children with heart disease. Additional funding came from Gurine and John Gall. The lodge comfortably sleeps 28 people.

Spokes & Wheels Bike Garage

Spokes & Wheels was built in memory of Brett & Rachel Wiskow, Fritz & Dorothy Wilson, and Norman & Louise Wiskow. Twenty-nine family members and friends, spanning four generations, formed a volunteer construction crew and completed the recreational-equipment storage building in one weekend.

K & A Nature Center

The K & A Nature Center was given in loving memory of Clayton & Francis Keister and Don & Murldean Austin by their children, Richard & Sharon Keister. The gift was given with the conviction that ordinary people with a passion for organizations which help make kids' lives better can, by their actions, encourage others to become involved, as well. Equipment and supplies for the Nature Center were donated in memory of Natalie Van Horst with the words "Natalie, our free spirit, is now a star watching over us."

Also constructed during *Rebuilding for Good* were the Director's Residence; a free-standing garage and workshop which provides unheated storage and a heated workshop; a storage garage addition donated by Dan and Sandi Thorson; and a Gazebo which provides a sheltered picnic area.

On occasion, the campers have been known
to end their camp session with a fully-dressed
plunge in the lake.

Resources

From Dream to Reality

From Camp Knutson Archives

    Board of Charities - Evangelical Lutheran Church. *Board Minutes* 1954 – 67.

    Camp Knutson Advisory Council. *Council Minutes* 1977 – 79.

    Camp Knutson Dedication Program. "Harold and Jeannette Holm Knutson biographies." 23 Aug. 1953

    Dahlen, Rev. Magnes. "A Summer Retreat to Gladden the Heart." *Radio Broadcast Script* 14 Aug. 1953

    Dahlen, Rev. Magnes. "A 'Bethesda by the Sea.'" *Lutheran Herald* 6 Oct. 1953: 899–91.

    Division of Social Service - American Lutheran Church. *Board Minutes* 1973 – 77.

Franklin, Robert. "Camp for Special-Needs Children Debating Whether to Sell or Stay."
    Star Tribune, Minneapolis 27 Dec. 1998: B1, 4.

Changing Times and Opening Doors

From Lutheran Social Service Archives

    LSS Board of Directors. "Board Minutes." LSS archives 10–11 Sept. 1998

    Moilanen, Mark. "Utilization of Camp Knutson" *Consultation Report* 1 Dec. 1998

    LSS Board of Directors. "Feasibility Study: Executive Summary." LSS archives 5 Jan. 1999.

    Camp Knutson Task Force. *Summary* 5 Jan. 1999.

    LSS Board of Directors. "LSS Board Votes to Redevelop Camp Knutson." *News Release* LSS archives 8 Jan. 1999

    LSS Booklet. "Camp Knutson: "Continuing the Dream." *Re-Dedication Ceremony* 23 Aug. 2000

    Camp Knutson-Camp Happenings. "Rebuilding for Good." *Annual Report* 2002.

    Paul Bunyon Regional Auxiliary of Lutheran Social Service. "Auxiliary Minutes." Camp Knutson archives 1976 – 1998

Dufour, Christine. "Camp Hosts Children With Skin Disease." *Brainerd Daily Dispatch* 27 Aug. 1997:

Frank, Peter. "Charter School Goes to Camp Knutson." *Lake Country Echo* 27 Jul. 2000: 4

Hanson, Linda. "Changing Lives." *Duluth News Tribune* 13 Aug. 2000: F1,7.

Lamb, Lynette. "No Putdowns Allowed." *The Lutheran* July 2000 p. 40–42.

Larson, Beth. "Every Quilt Has A Story." *Lake Country Echo* 19 Aug. 2004: A2

Ryan, Betty. "Future of Camp Knutson." *Lake Country Echo* 10 Oct. 1991: 1,6.

Ryan, Betty. "Whitefish Camp May Be Saved From Selling Block." *Lake Country Echo* 16 Jan. 1992: 1,6.
Ryan, Betty. "Deja Vu." *Lake Country Echo* 19 Nov. 1998: 1,6
Ryan, Betty. "Camp Knutson Won't Be Sold." *Lake Country Echo* 14 Jan. 1999: 1,6.
Ryan, Betty. "Five Year Building Plan." *Lake Country Echo* 1 Apr. 1999
Ryan, Betty. "Groundbreaking at Camp Knutson." *Lake Country Echo* 19 Oct. 1999. 1, 23
Ryan, Betty. "Camp Knutson, 50 Years of Serving Kids With Special Needs." *Lake Country Echo* 28 Aug. 2003: A20.
Tweed, Jodie. "Camp Marks 50 Years." *Brainerd Daily Dispatch* 27 Aug. 2003: N1.

Camp Knutson Today

Christenson, Kathryn. "A Different Kind of Summer Camp." *MetroLutheran* March 2003: 11.
Dahl, Mark V, MD, Roerig, Mary Jane, RN, Pride, Howard B., MD, and Rabinowitz, Linda K. "Camp Knutson: The First Three Years." *Journal of the American Academy of Dermatology.* Jul. 1996: 96, 98, 100.
Franklin, Robert. "Comfortable in Their Skin." *Star Tribune* Minneapolis 29 Jun. 1999: E1,2
Franklin, Robert. "Camp with Heart." *Star Tribune* Minneapolis 19 Aug, 2003: E1 – 8
Ryan, Betty. "Camp Knutson Has Always Been A Passion For Erickson." *Lake Country Echo* 28 Oct. 2010: A6,7.
Shwayder, Tor, MD. "Call of the Loon." *Journal of the American Medical Association.* 14 Oct. 1998:1221
Tomson, Ellen. "Happy Campers." *St. Paul Pioneer Press* 18 Jul. 2000: C1-2.
Tweed, Jodie. "Camp Caters to Autistic Children." *Brainerd Daily Dispatch* 6 Aug. 2000: A1, 6.
Websites:
    American Academy of Dermatology: Camp Little Pine & Camp Big Trout www. campdiscovery.org/
    Autism Society of Minnesota: Camp Hand in Hand www.ausm.org/
    Camp Benedict www.campbenedict.org/
    Camp Odayin www.campodayin.com
    Down Syndrome Camp www.downsyndromefoundation.org

The Work of Many

Camp Knutson Volunteers. Minutes and Miscellaneous Documents 2002-13. Camp Knutson Archives
LSS Annual Reports 2003 – 2013. LSS Archives
Ryan, Betty. "Slovak Church's Legacy Builds Camp Cabin." *Lake Country Echo* 29 Jun. 2000: 14.
Ryan, Betty. "Friends of Camp Knutson Celebrate." *Lake Country Echo* 1 June. 2001: 5
Ryan, Betty. "There's A Story Behind Every Building At Camp Knutson." *Lake Country Echo* 2011.